Attachment Theory, The Science of Successful Relationships, Authentic Love, Romance and Connection

Copyright Notice

No part of this book may be reproduced or transmitted in any form whatsoever, electronic, or mechanical, including photocopying, recording, or by any information storage or retrieval system without expressed written, dated and signed permission from the author. All copyrights are reserved.

Disclaimer

Reasonable care has been taken to ensure that the information presented in this book is accurate. However, the reader should understand that the information provided does not constitute legal, medical or professional advice of any kind.

No Liability: this product is supplied "as is" and without warranties. All warranties, express or implied, are hereby disclaimed. Use of this product constitutes acceptance of the "No Liability" policy. If you do not agree with this policy, you are not permitted to use or distribute this product.

We shall not be liable for any losses or damages whatsoever (including, without limitation, consequential loss or damage) directly or indirectly arising from the use of this product.

Claim your FREE Audiobook Now

<u>The Confident New You - Develop Your Confidence and Start Living the Life You Deserve</u>

Do you get lost for words around other people, or do you suffer from social anxiety? Are you more concerned about how you look to other people?

If your confidence is always holding you back from achieving what you really want in your life, or if you have always been super shy with no confidence then read on.

You're about to discover how to be confident in any situation. Find out how to make a great first impression and keep the conversation going, without appearing awkward.

Learn to stop thinking negatively about yourself and conquer your fears to gain unstoppable confidence at anything. Even if you don't have low confidence, you can always benefit from improved confidence - there are always greater heights to reach.

THE CONFIDENT NEW YOU

DEVELOP YOUR CONFIDENCE AND START LIVING THE LIFE YOU DESERVE

DARCY CARTER

TABLE OF CONTENTS

Description

Introduction

Chapter 1 The Basics of Attachment Theory

Chapter 2 Yourself and the Other You

Chapter 3 Understanding Your Partner

The Brain-to-Brain Connection of Attunement

Understanding Your Partner's Reactions to Your Anxiety

Chapter 4 Connections with Toddlers: Encouraging Safe Exploration

Chapter 5 Creating a Sense of Felt Safety

Chapter 6 Creating a Toddler-Friendly Home:

Chapter 7 The Interplay of Parent–Child Relationships

Chapter 8 Insecure, Dismissive, and Avoidant Attachment

Chapter 9 Creating a Higher Sense of Intimacy with Your Partner

Chapter 10 Tips for Improving Communication Between Couples

Chapter 11 Giving is Being

Chapter 12 Changing How You Handle Conflict

Chapter 13 Relationship Mistakes You Don't Want to Repeat

Chapter 14 Self-Work

Conclusion

DESCRIPTION

There are different kinds of attachment relationships, but the optimal one we hope to establish is called "secure attachment." Secure attachment is a deep and enduring emotional bond between a child and an adult who is consistently physically available, who shares a warm reciprocal relationship of intimacy, and assumes responsibility for the well-being of the child.

We all want to be connected to our children. In those first moments of life, we gaze into the face of our newborn and imagine the life we'll have together. The infant gazes back at the face that will offer enduring comfort and ongoing joy and delight throughout the life of the child.

We envision their first word, their first day of school, their first date, or their graduation from high school. We think about their birthdays and celebrations, the good-night hugs and kisses, and joy that we'll share.

No one looks at their newborn and envisions a four-year-old getting kicked out of childcare because of his aggressive behavior, or a sullen ten-year-old who won't talk because he is obsessed with video games, or the rebellious teenager getting his hands on the car keys and wrecking the family car.

You just picked the right book that will steer your relationships in the right direction. Your attachments will never be the same, it will help you enhance every area of your life and you will appreciate life and the people around you more.

This guide will take you through various attachments and how they work, ways to improve your relationship by understanding your partner better and working on the flaws to make a better and a happy marriage. Creating better bonds with your toddler and children for a happy family.

Thanks for downloading this book. It's my firm belief that it will provide you with all the answers to your questions.

INTRODUCTION

We envision a life of connection and the joy that intimate relationships bring. The drive to connect is in our DNA and part of what it means to be made in the image of God. We all long to share a lasting connection with our kids, and they long to share a lasting connection with us.

Sometimes, the biological bond and attachment are confused as the same thing. A biological bond is present at the moment of conception. A secure attachment is a connection that grows as a result of positive and consistent experiences with Mom and Dad.

God has exquisitely designed us in such a way as to jump-start the love relationship between a child and a parent even before we lay eyes on our baby. Some moms report that they have warm fuzzy feelings toward their child the moment they know they are pregnant. Others report that it happens when they see the first ultrasound or feel the first kick. At whatever point the baby becomes a reality, Mom begins to joyfully anticipate the infant's arrival and a mental image of the child begins to unfold—this little person soon to be placed in her arms.

Parents begin to imagine what the baby will look like, what family traits will be passed down, and what they will enjoy doing together. These positive images translate into a positive prenatal environment.

Every emotion a mom feels has a corresponding neurochemical cocktail that is also experienced by the developing child. When a mom carries positive images and looks forward to the birth of her baby, this contributes to a healthy intrauterine environment.

The baby who is joyfully anticipated knows he is wanted the moment he is born. Psychiatrist, Curt Thompson says, "Every child is born looking for someone looking for him." To be wanted and "looked for" is the birthright of every child. On the other hand, there are babies who were a "mistake." The birth control failed. The child was conceived in the context of an extramarital affair, or in a drunken stupor, or as a result of rape. To be unwanted is toxic to the human soul.

CHAPTER 1
The Basics of Attachment Theory

One of the ways we can help answer our questions is to look at something called attachment theory. I first read about adult attachment a few years ago, but it seemed like some psychological mumbo jumbo that didn't have much bearing on my day to day life. After revisiting the concept more recently it was like a light bulb went off in my head and everything was illuminated. I began to look at ALL of my past relationships through the attachment theory lenses, which helped me create emotional distance and understand some of the dynamics that I had previously thought were due to a flaw within myself.

John Bowlby, a British psychologist pioneered research into how and why infants attached to their primary caregivers, and how the caregivers' responses affected the behavior of the infant. Two of his main discoveries were that infants attached out of necessity to survive, and that they were stuck with whatever caregiver they had, whether that person was responsive to their needs or not .

Building on Bowlby's work, another psychologist, Mary Arnsworth, developed a specific study, the Strange Situation Test, and posited that there were four different ways that infants attached to their caregivers , called attachment styles .

In the 1980s, the infant attachment style research was expanded to include adults and how they attach in romantic relationships. These styles are called adult attachment styles.

Now that we have that bit of history out of the way, let's look at the four different attachment styles. You may see these worded a little differently depending on the source, but the essentials for each category are the same. Here are the hallmarks of each style.

Secure

Secure attachment is what it sounds like. These people are open and loving, and aren't preoccupied with relationships. In childhood, their caregivers were attentive and responsive to their needs most of the time. They were allowed to safely explore the world and learned to rely on themselves and those around them. They generally believe that others are trustworthy and caring, and therefore when faced with conflict within a relationship, they don't overreact or assume the worst of the other person. This is the gold standard of attachment styles.

Avoidant

Avoidant people are just that, avoidant. They keep their partner at arm's length, detest real intimacy, and are very judgemental of their significant others. They keep secrets, send mixed signals, and always keep an escape route open in relationships. In childhood their caregivers were mostly unresponsive, dismissive, and distant. They learned not to rely on others and to repress their emotions. They don't open up, don't want to be trapped, and never seem to be affected by relationship issues.

Anxious

These people (most likely you and me) desire closeness in a relationship. They are insecure, and worried that the other person will leave them or stop loving them. They are very sensitive to their partner's moods, get attached quickly, and when anxious, do and say things they later regret. In childhood their caregivers were inconsistent, sometimes distant and unresponsive, and other times invasive and over protective. These people always feel like there is something wrong with them in the relationship. They are often preoccupied with their relationships, and can't stop thinking about their partners.

Disorganized

This style is called disorganized because unlike the other styles, these people don't follow a pattern. They exhibit traits of both anxious and avoidant. They want to be close in a relationship, but feel trapped when they are. They judge their partners, yet they and feel that something is wrong with themselves. They don't open up, but in a fit of anxiety, they overshare. They don't show that they are affected by a relationship, but inside, they are preoccupied with it. In childhood these children often experienced neglect or abuse and had caregivers who were violent and unpredictable.

It is important to note that although attachment styles start in infancy, they are not set in stone. Traumatic events in one's life can shift a person from secure to one of the insecure attachment types. Losing a parent, being sexually assaulted, or any number of negative experiences can affect how we attach in relationships. Conversely, caregivers who choose to heal themselves and consciously change their abusive, anxious, or otherwise non-secure ways of parenting can have a positive impact on children who may have begun as anxious, avoidant, or disorganized attached.

With this basic information, you can start to think about your own style and those of your past partners. Chances are, if you are anxious, you've been with many avoidants. If you're anything like me, you're reading the secure description and thinking I didn't even know there were people like that out there! But rest assured that in actuality, about half of the population have a secure attachment style, so there is hope.

CHAPTER 2

Yourself and the Other You

For many years I asked myself, am I in the right relationship? Is this relationship good for me? Am I good to my partner? At this point in my life, after many realizations have taken place, I wonder: was I seeing myself separate from my own relationship?

When you analyze the question my mind was asking above, can you see the two entities? Moreover, can you see how I was asking if the relationship was providing something to me? Is this relationship good to me?

I had no idea how I behaved in relationships. Had you actually stopped me and asked me about my beliefs, I would have come up with a really amazing concept for what a relationship is. Yet, that's not how my mind was responding to it. I would truly feel the heavenly concept of love within. But I could not see how my behavior would make me and others miserable. Even when attempting to correspond with my true beliefs.

I was waiting for the relationship to define me, and it did. Constantly. That means the state of the relationship defined my mood, my emotional state, and what I was able to happily give. When the relationship was not at its best, if those involved are not there to catch it, how could it survive?

I struggled to show up. I did, or at least I gave every piece of what I did not have, to show up. I believe I did show up many times, however, I did not enjoy it for the most part. If I served, I needed a response and feedback almost immediately. And of course, I did! I had given my last two cents. I needed a refund. And quick.

Serving others turned into a painful process. When I did, I would empty out instantly. I would stay there expecting, standing, hoping to be filled back. Like an empty bucket of shame.

I can clearly identify the pain right now. I can, with absolute certainty, identify what really hurt in those moments.

It hurt not feeling emotionally able to give to the person I loved, when it was what I wanted the most.

So here is a divine child of God struggling to love. Wanting to love and give, wringing every single drop from a heart that was empty.

Normally, an emotionally fit person in this situation would recognize there is an empty bucket there and say: Okay, I need to go fill this up, so I can serve you. I have to stop, go take care of myself, put my oxygen mask on, before I can be there for you.

But here is the essence of the matter. I did not recognize the lack as a problem within myself, but a problem in others.

Make abundance within yourself a prerequisite for your relationships.

Your lack cannot be filled from an external source.

I was no one without the acceptance and validation of my partner. I could not stay still. I was anxious. I was terrified of my own state, of being alone with my thoughts. These thoughts that talked to me about what I had lived by and not who I was inside. I was terrified of not becoming who I heard I had to be, forgetting a small but very critical detail:

I should have set out myself to accomplish things in life, and not to be someone in life, for I already was. I had always been whole and nothing was ever missing.

This pattern was present my whole life, in all of my relationships. Romantically, in friendships. In some, stronger than others. But definitely more pronounced as I approached the realization of my absolute lack of self-love.

My marriage set me on the path for this transformation to take place. It gave me the necessary tools to experience my lack of self-love, over and over, and its consequences. Had I had an understanding and loving wife; I would still be light years away from the deepest realization of my life.

Many individuals already have an amazing mate. I had the perfect partner for evolutionary purposes, let's put it that way. I've shared these lessons with hope that it can inspire your heart to start searching for your ultimate fulfillment and true, giving love.

It took me a long time to realize my lacking. My mind, which still struggles with accepting the perfection of the universe, believes that if I had consciously known what I lacked, then I could have chosen to replenish sooner.

I would have built self-standards to be filled differently, in a loving way, or to step out with a little less overall damage. However, I feel not even one second was wasted. Every single experience had a purpose. All those experiences were used to be part of a destiny-changing decision.

Yet, I did not know I didn't love myself until I made the switch right in front of 5,000 other loving humans. When I experienced the love of so many others in the very moment I despised myself the most, it was in that moment I came to realize what was preventing me from living. It was my own neglect of my humanity.

How would our relationships change if we could see them as catalyzers to our wholeness and our contribution to the world?

The dominant question when facing a challenge was to doubt my partner, or the relationship itself: Is this relationship good for me?

What if we could ask a different question from now on instead?

How can I share even more the love and abundance that naturally occurs in my heart, in this moment?

Words of Wisdom

Stop for a moment.

Look at the relationships in your life. Is there any relationship that brings you pain, maybe discomfort? Are there any relationships you are hoping to change, improve or transform?

Improving our relationships is great. But consider that any change outside of your core and your emotional state is a change that will add anxiety to your life. Controlling anything external to you will add a great deal of stress to how you think and project toward yourself and others.

If we attach our realization to external agents, we might experience instantaneous successes and moments of pleasure, but would we experience fulfillment?

I see you.

I do not doubt your definition of love and relationship is quite beautiful and giving. We can love and even give our life for someone we love, yet fail to be happy ourselves. As a result, those who love us would also suffer. It's a no-winners game.

I invite you to look at how you define relationships and how much you really enjoy acting on that definition. Is it fulfilling? Or do you struggle keeping up with the definition of love you have set up for yourself? If you only have control of yourself (and partially!), can you really bet your daily energy on how the other person is having their day? Maybe only you exist in the universe, and me, and everyone, by ourselves. And from each of our solo perspectives everyone is an agent of change in each other's lives.

Thank the people in your life for being how they are. They will heal as you heal, they will have their own time to meet their lessons. Others will come who will challenge you with new lessons in life.

If you happen to lose perspective for a minute, look around you. Who surrounds you? Who are they? What challenges are you facing? Relationships are a way to serve others in their own destinies.

If you love others, grow so you can set them free.

The deepest proof of love you can truly give is to act from your place of center and balance. It is a signal to the universe that you are ready to enter someone else's world, and make it worthwhile. If you do not love yourself, and you are in the search for the true you, the universe will serve you by bringing interactions with others who have the same need and even in a more pronounced way. It will bring you a mirror, bigger and clearer every time along the way.

Have you ever been to the optometrist where they show you the letters and numbers and ask you if you can see it now? And you can't? And they change the lens and repeat the question: can you see it now?

The lenses are our experiences. They get harder and harder for us to understand the picture we need to see of ourselves, and be able to decode it, read it, understand it.

Funny enough, I just got glasses.

Physical ones and emotional ones.

Get yours. Put them on.

Share yourself with others wearing them. Sharing who you really are is interacting from a vision and a concept of others that sometimes they cannot see. It is possible you will see two in every person you interact with. You might see their monster and their higher being. Their human nature, their lessons, and their heavenly presence. Your role is to interact with their higher selves, and love and appreciate their humanity.

Do not engage negatively with the part of themselves they do not love.

Appreciate it, forgive it, and walk away from that door.

Face the other door, their heart.

Knock.

If they do not see their divinity, you must understand the shortest path to their awakening is just your presence. Gracefully wait at the door, with a full heart. Throwing rocks against that door will only thicken it, will only trigger more protection. Inside, there is a weak and thin being who is terrified to walk out. Only peace and love will make it safe to do so.

Wait for their bloom on the side of the door with open arms and a rose in your heart.

CHAPTER 3

Understanding Your Partner

This chapter provides a foundation on which you can begin to recognize and repair the disconnect that may exist between you and your partner and to shift the overall dynamic of your relationship.

You may feel that if your partner really loved you, she would intuitively know how to respond to your needs and would always give you the support that you want. While this is an understandable desire, sadly it's more fantasy than likelihood. Love doesn't automatically lead to understanding or to the ability to recognize and respond sensitively to one another's needs. This is especially true when chronic anxiety enters the picture.

Lauren, a classic worrier, realized that her anxiety was hurting her marriage. Like others with generalized anxiety disorder, she was frequently overwhelmed by anticipatory anxiety and spent much of her time ruminating on possible catastrophes. She was particularly worried about her only child, Anna. Her most recent worry was about which school would be best for Anna, who was entering kindergarten in the fall. When her sister asked Lauren what Lauren's husband thought about the options, Lauren just shook her head.

"It's always the same with Rob. No matter what I'm worried about, he refuses to even consider my concerns. So many things could go wrong. I've heard that one of the kindergarten teachers at the neighborhood school is really mean. What if Anna gets her as a teacher? If Anna starts off on the wrong foot, she might hate school forever. This could completely color the trajectory of her entire education. But when I say this, Rob just rolls his eyes and says I'm making mountains out of molehills, that Anna is a happy, easygoing little girl and will be fine wherever she goes—period, end of conversation. He won't take anything I say seriously. And then when I keep on him about it, he either gets annoyed or shuts down and refuses to talk with me at all.

"His logical engineer's mind used to be one of the things that I loved and appreciated about him. He's always so calm about everything. Everything with him can be factored into some logical analysis. But now it's driving me crazy; everything is just logic to him. Any concern I have is met with this brick wall of reason and tossed aside.

"It feels as if he doesn't care about my thoughts—or me—at all. I don't think he even understands where I'm coming from. I used to think my anxiety was the problem, but now I think it's my marriage too. It's as if I don't have a wife anymore—or at least, this isn't what I wanted when I envisioned going through my life with a partner."

We have heard countless client's express frustrations similar to Lauren's. Their pain of not feeling understood and cared for by the one they love becomes a palpable presence in the therapy room. Of course, we all want to be understood, especially by the one we love. Unfortunately, struggles with empathy and support for one another are common in committed relationships. This is particularly the case, however, in relationships in which one partner has an anxiety disorder or heightened anxiety.

In this chapter, you'll gain an understanding of the neuroscience of connection and learn some of the ways connection can be disrupted when one partner has a chronic anxiety disorder. You will also gain a greater understanding of your partner's responses to your anxiety. But first, let's try to get our heads around the brain.

The Neurobiology of Connection

Neurologically, the impasse between you and your partner makes perfect sense. When you are flooded with anxiety and your partner isn't, you and your partner are actually "speaking" from different places in your brains. To understand this, let's look at how the brain works.

The Brain-to-Brain Connection of Attunement

Attunement, being intellectually and emotionally in sync with one another, is crucial to relationships at every developmental stage. The opposite of isolation, attunement encompasses a sense of relatedness: shared interest, curiosity, and understanding. Attunement is first achieved during infancy through an entirely nonverbal language of emotions. It is a language of shared looks and glances, shared smiles, soothing touch, and sounds of laughter and contentment. In the first year of life, we learn a rich, complex language of connection, even before we learn to speak. It is also a shared language of sorrow or discomfort. Even as we grow older and develop the capacity to communicate through the spoken word, attunement continues to be conveyed largely nonverbally. Words barely scratch the surface when compared to the depth of compassion and care that can be felt through a mutual gaze or through the comforting touch or sympathetic body posture of an attuned other.

When two individuals are in attunement through this complex web of verbal and nonverbal interaction, they are emotionally on the same page. They experience emotional resonance: emotionally, they are humming the same tune. This emotional resonance, or connection, is present because various structures within the midbrain, forebrain, and even hindbrain of the attuned individuals are in sync. Thus when you and your partner are in attunement, many emotion-based centers in your midbrains are literally firing in similar patterns in response to one another.

Attunement does not, however, suggest that your emotions are identical. When an infant express distress by crying, for example, an attuned caregiver does not become distraught to match the feelings of the baby. The caregiver approaches the infant softly and calmly, recognizing and meeting the baby's needs for comfort and support. In the same way, if you are stressed, you might reach out to your partner for support. Your partner doesn't show support by becoming as stressed as you are. An attuned partner ideally provides you with care and attention to help you to restore an inner sense of well-being.

Anxiety and Ruptures in Attunement

When you become overwhelmed with anxiety, your emotion-based midbrain goes into hyperdrive, and you become more or less cut off from your forebrain's rational, analytical input. You begin to speak the language of pure emotion and are unable to get in sync with your partner, who has more access to her forebrain. When your emotions are revved, it's very hard, without your newly acquired skills of this book, to reengage your forebrain, calm your anxious emotions, and regain the attunement and emotional connection. Attunement requires a balance of forebrain and midbrain activity. This means that the midbrain needs to be functioning at optimal levels of activation, where you are able to experience emotion without being overtaken by it. This, of course, is not the case when you are flooded with anxiety.

Again, imagine that you are experiencing overpowering feelings of fear and worry, and that you go to your partner for support. Regardless of your partner's response, without a balance of midbrain and forebrain activation, the sense of safety and well-being that accompanies attuned connection will be lacking. Even the most responsive partner will be unable to provide the sense of well-being that your anxiety disorder has taken from you.

In the absence of a sense of comfort through connection, it's easy to feel that your partner isn't "there" for you, to feel angry, and to withdraw even further, widening the gulf that already exists. Your focus narrows to your own thoughts, body responses, and decisions, and then to your increased isolation. In the face of these overwhelming stressors, it's understandable that you would withdraw. This inner focus can lead you to lose sight of your partner's feelings and thus fall farther away from the sense of connection that you desire.

Now that you have learned the anxiety-regulating techniques presented in part 1, you are equipped to begin to bridge the gulf that may have developed between you and your partner. You can now reestablish the midbrain-forebrain communication that opens the way for the attuned connection that was lost when you were flooded by anxiety. Now you can broaden the focus of your recovery to include your interactions with your partner and change them for the better.

The first step in this process is to gain an understanding of your partner's responses and reactions to your anxiety. Once you develop a broader understanding of these reactions and responses, you will be better able to empathize with your partner and alter your communication patterns.

Understanding Your Partner's Reactions to Your Anxiety

The most effective way to better understand your partner's reactions to your anxiety—the goal of this section—is to temporarily shift your attention from yourself to your partner's inner experience. Throughout our years of clinical practice, we have found that partners' reactions typically take one or some combination of three modes: the *appeal*, the *attack*, and the *retreat*. Each person is different, but you are likely to find your partner in the following descriptions.

The Appeal: Speaking the Language of Reason

Most commonly, partners first react to your anxiety by trying to help you see that your fears are illogical. Recall that when you are flooded with anxiety, your partner is much more in touch with the logical forebrain than you are. So your partner's first impulse may be to appeal to your sense of reason. Partners often think that with logic, you'll snap out of it and feel better. But as you have learned, rational arguments are not powerful enough to defuse your anxiety.

Put yourself in your partner's shoes. Imagine that your typical roles are reversed: your partner is overwhelmed with anxiety and has come to you for help and support. You don't want your partner to suffer. Assuming that you're not overwhelmed with emotion yourself, you will most likely offer a suggestion based on a logical appraisal of the situation. But your well-intended support doesn't even put a dent in your partner's anxiety. It's understandable that you feel frustrated with yourself for being unable to help, with your partner for not benefiting from your well-intended advice, and with the fact that you live with someone who is chronically anxious.

Continue to imagine yourself in your partner's shoes. Your frustration may also intensify when you try to reestablish an attuned connection with your anxious partner. Indeed, reestablishing this connection probably feels more urgent because your partner is in a great deal of distress. But this effort to connect won't succeed, because the communication between your partner's midbrain and forebrain has been interrupted by your partner's intense emotions. The result is that you don't feel any attuned connection with your anxious partner. You feel isolated—alone. What's more, you feel that all your well-intentioned efforts at connection have failed.

Now step back into your own shoes and remember your own repeated experiences of isolation, when you have been flooded with anxiety and discouraged that your partner couldn't connect with you. At those moments, your partner may have been trying to establish the very connection you desired. And your partner may have felt frustration and a similar sense of isolation when the connection wasn't made. All of this mounting frustration and failure to connect can sometimes set the stage for a shift into the attack or the retreat.

The Attack: Reacting Emotionally

Frustrated by his inability to calm you down and reestablish connection, your partner may become emotional. Reason may be replaced with anger, disappointment, or even rage. Harsh words and blame are common in this mode of reacting. Your partner might say that you should be able to deal with your anxiety on your own, that you are too dependent, or that he is tired of constantly having to deal with your anxiety. You might feel as if your partner is belittling you for anxiety that you can't control. Past and ongoing disputes between you might enter the argument here, adding fuel to the fire.

When your partner is on the attack, neither of you is calm or in a frame of mind to give or receive support. Your interaction is intense, but it won't foster mutual connection. Rather, it fosters increasing isolation and hurt.

The Retreat: Sensing Defeat and Seeking Isolation

In sharp contrast to the attack, the retreat mode is marked by a *lack* of interaction. Your partner may retreat emotionally or physically, or both, in an effort to get away from the conflict or your anxiety. While the retreat may feel like the calm after the storm (especially if it follows the attack), the isolation and loss of connection you both experience can be just as devastating as the more active conflict of the attack.

You may feel as if your partner, in retreat mode, is light-years away. Even if you are in the same room, the distance between you couldn't seem greater. Whether your partner holds a tight-lipped silence that stems from anger or goes emotionally numb and fails to connect, the retreat creates a stalemate. The silence can be just as hurtful and harmful as a heated exchange if the climate of disconnect between the two of you is allowed to linger.

While it's common to shift from one mode of reacting to the next sequentially, everyone is different and responds to her partner's intense anxiety differently. An awareness of the three types of reactions provides you with a better understanding of your partner's responses to your anxiety. It allows you to begin to step back from your own inner experience to gain a broader appreciation of the rifts in connection between you and your partner. There are many ways to reinforce your newfound larger perspective on the disconnect you often feel with your partner.

CHAPTER 4

Connections with Toddlers: Encouraging Safe Exploration

There is nothing more fun and fascinating than a toddler! Their newfound mobility, emerging personality, and language skills make the toddler a delightful little person to be with. The toddler years are typically defined as the period between 18 and 36 months. Despite the fact that language skills are still limited, toddlers are very adept at making their wishes, needs, and desires clearly known.

The reciprocal nature of the attachment bond becomes even stronger as the toddler is now able to actively seek proximity to Mom and Dad and initiate physical affection and interaction. Despite the increase in language, much of the communication between toddlers and their parents continues to be nonverbal. Mom and Dad's facial expressions continue to be an important component in orienting the child to his world.

The cute and cuddly infant-turned-toddler becomes a whirlwind of perpetual motion, climbing on everything, and insisting on doing things his own way. He empties the kitchen cabinets of the pots and pans, unrolls the toilet paper, and laughs while doing it. The living room furniture is his jungle gym. He throws temper tantrums when he doesn't get his way and "no, me, mine" become his favorite words. This is why many refer to the toddler years as the "terrible twos."

So what is going on here? Do these really have to be "terrible" years? Are these behaviors a mark of the toddler's rebellious nature? Is it willful defiance, or could it be something else?

The behavior of the toddler can be easily misunderstood if we do not look through the lens of child development. These years can truly be the "terrific twos" and a time of awe and wonder as Mom and Dad watch the development of their child. So how do we parent toddlers well and continue to strengthen the emotional connection?

CHAPTER 5

Creating a Sense of Felt Safety

Emotional Availability:

Toddlers are highly emotional little people and sometimes experience strong feelings that can overwhelm them. The manner in which Mom or Dad responds to their emotions is important. When parents respond to, and don't avoid, the intense anger and frustration of a toddler with a calming and supportive presence, it reassures the toddler that Mom and Dad are psychologically big enough to take care of him.

The toddler comes to realize, "The world isn't going to fall apart when I do. Mom and Dad aren't going to come undone when I do. Mom and Dad are big enough to keep me safe."

If a parent reacts to a toddler's temper tantrum with anger, frustration, or withdrawal, the child experiences fear and anxiety. If Mom and Dad can't handle my big emotions, then, how can I?

This is why predictability is so crucial for your child—even when it's difficult for you, and especially when it's difficult for you.

Predictability:

The brain hates chaos and unpredictability. By the time the child reaches toddlerhood, his biological rhythms with regard to eating, sleeping, waking, and playing have assimilated into the schedule of the family. Creating a sense of routine and "sameness" helps the toddler feel safe.

Establishing routines can make life run more smoothly for the entire family. This allows both parents and children to invest their emotional energies in connecting. The morning routine is extremely important, especially if both parents are working and the toddler is in childcare. How families begin the day sets the emotional tone for the entire day. Some things to think about:

- How do I awaken my toddler? Do I stand in the kitchen and shout? Or yell from the bottom of the stairs? Do they awaken on their own? If so, how do I respond to them when they come pitter patting into my room and wake me up?

- Do I make time to cuddle, read, or simply hold my toddler for a few minutes? Or am I in a chaotic rush to get out the door?

- How do I decide what my toddler is going to wear? Do I give her two choices the night before and have it laid out? Or, do I tell my child what she is going to wear as we are getting dressed? Am I scrambling around the house looking for clean clothes, thereby stressing myself out as well as my child?

- How and when do we eat breakfast? Do we eat before we get dressed? After we get dressed? How do we decide what to eat? Do I have a routine menu? Do I grab the first thing I see in the cabinet? Do I give my toddler a choice between two things, or do I decide for him?

- • What is the bedtime routine? Do we eat snack or read a story before or after we take a bath? Do I lie beside them or expect them to go to sleep on their own? Do both Mom and Dad play a part in bedtime routines with each child, or do we "divide and conquer?"

I struggled with "sameness" and predictability when my children were young. Because of my wife's quadriplegia, medical emergencies happened on a regular basis. Our youngest daughter also experienced serious medical issues at age two. There were many disruptions to our daily routine that were beyond my control. I strived to keep our morning and bedtime routines the same. If we could at least begin and end the day with a sense of predictability, it made our lives easier—and my children had at least some sense of normalcy.

It's also important to realize that predictability isn't necessarily about clock time. We got up and went to bed approximately at the same time, but we weren't militant about the clock. If a neighbor came by and bedtime was delayed twenty minutes, it was all good. Predictability was more about doing the same things in the same order, day in and day out.

I recently explained this to a dad who was recently discharged from the military. We were talking about clock time vs. predictability of events. His face immediately brightened and he said, "Oh, I get it. In the military, we call it event planning. We may not know the time a particular event takes place, but we always know the order in which it plays out." Event planning helps all children feel safe.

Touch:

Touch continues to be an important form of connection with toddlers. Their increasing mobility enables them to initiate and seek out contact and playful touch. They crawl into Mom and Dad's lap, wrap themselves around your leg, crawl in bed with you, pinch your nose, tickle your chin, and throw their arms around you in a bear hug.

Responding with warmth and affection is natural for most parents. There is nothing that makes my heart happy like getting a hug from my two-year-old grandson. There is just something about the unbridled affection of a toddler that brings joy to the soul and hope to keep on keeping on—no matter how hard life can be. It's the ultimate reward for all the inconveniences parenting sometimes brings.

If you find yourself uncomfortable with giving or receiving touch from your child, it's important to look at your own childhood and think about the messages that were communicated to you about touch. Some families are very touchy-feely, and others rarely touch at all.

A friend related that she had no memories of being hugged or touched as a child by either one of her parents. When she had her first baby, she found herself weeping one day as she sat and rocked her newborn. At first she thought she was crazy, but she found herself thinking over and over, How could a mom not hug her child? She found that unfathomable.

This was the first time it occurred to her that she had no memories of being touched by her parents. She reported that over the years as she rocked, hugged, and cuddled with her children, she found healing and discovered the joy and pleasure of physical closeness.

As time went on, she learned more about the history of her parents—the hardships and challenges they faced in their own childhood. The more she learned about her own family history, the more it made sense that touch was not part of the dynamic of her family of origin. But, as often happens, this wound that she felt earlier slowly began to heal as she gave her children what she never had.

In giving, she found healing. You can, too. Healing can also be found in playfulness.

Simple childhood games such as Pat-a-Cake, This Little Piggy, and Peek-a-Boo not only provide playful touch, but also build important cognitive skills. Piggyback rides, blowing raspberries on tummies, and riding on a parent's shoulders are fun ways of physically connecting. Toddlers beckon parents to chase them. They flop into your lap while you read, and they invite you to roughhouse.

Infant massage continues to be valuable as the child moves in toddler stage. And the massage strokes used on smaller children can be adapted for a physically larger child. By the time a child reaches toddlerhood, massage may become a regular and routine part of the day.

Toddlers love to sit with Mom and Dad to read books. Rocking, cuddling, and snuggling together build strong connections. Making meaningful touch a part of your daily routine is important to a child's development.

Tone of Voice:

Our tone of voice is another important way of creating a sense of felt safety, just as it did in infancy. Many of us continue to use the language of "mother-ese" with our toddlers.

However, with their growing sense of autonomy, toddlers increasingly engage in activities and behaviors that require the imposition of limits and elicit a stern "no" from Mom and Dad. Toddlers dump out the trash can, unroll the toilet paper, and empty the cabinets at the most inconvenient times. At the end of the day, parents are often exhausted from trying to meet the demands of parenthood and work. They can find themselves speaking in a harsh tone of voice that can sound loud and demanding.

It's always okay to be firm but never okay to be harsh. We send powerful messages to children simply through our tone. Our tone of voice is interpreted and perceived at a very unconscious level and either creates a sense of safety or fear.

When I want to set firm limits and communicate a sense that "I mean business" without frightening the child, I find it helpful to think in terms of lowering the tone of my voice and slowing my words down. It's not scary, and it's not harsh. And it sends a very clear message to the child's brain: I mean what I say.

If we speak to toddlers in a harsh tone of voice on a consistent basis, they will live in a persistent state of fear. Fear creates disconnection.

Eye Contact:

As toddlers grow in their autonomy and test the limits of their own power and the boundaries that are set for them, our feelings may fluctuate throughout the day. Fortunately, their cuteness factor can offset the irritation that can arise when they climb on the kitchen counter for the tenth time. But sometimes, in moments of high stress or fatigue, our feelings spill over. We might not verbalize anything, but our face says it all.

Our eyes are particularly reflective of how we feel. Soft eyes communicate love and acceptance. Bright, shining eyes portray joy. A hard, steely glare communicates anger and rejection. The eyes never lie. Toddlers are always watching and attuning to the face of Mom and Dad to determine what is acceptable and what is not. The watchfulness of toddlers plays a huge role in the development of conscience.

The child pulls the cat's tail and immediately checks Mom's facial expression or Dad's reaction. They pick up the potted plant and prepare to throw it. Dad leaps from his chair to retrieve it with a look of "Oh no, don't you dare." The toddler receives the message loud and clear that his behavior is not okay.

CHAPTER 6

Creating a Toddler-Friendly Home:

Notice that the title of this section isn't, "Creating a Toddler Dominated Home." There is a vast difference between a home that is child friendly and one that is dominated by a child of any age.

Children are born with a God-given desire to explore and master their world. They come packaged with an enormous curiosity to figure out how things work. This is how they learn. This is how they grow. The inquisitiveness of a toddler and his propensity to "get into everything" is not a sign of rebellion or "naughty" behavior. It is a mark of God's design.

This is important to grasp because if I view the inquisitiveness of the toddler and his propensity to make messes as evidence of his disobedience then I am likely to respond in a punitive manner. This will not only squelch his curiosity, but also undermine the emotional connection that I am striving to develop. The Scriptures say, "Train up a child in the way he should go, and when he is old, he will not depart from it." If we look at the original text, this verse says, "Train up a child in the way he is bent." Honoring what we know about child development is considering the "bent" of the child.

So the challenge is to balance the toddler's need to explore with the need to keep him safe—and to maintain our sanity. Of course I don't want my child to unroll the toilet paper every day, so I keep the bathroom door shut. I put the Tupperware and pots and pans in the lower cabinets and put the glass bakeware up high. I leave the inexpensive and unbreakable trinkets out on the coffee table but put the family heirlooms out of reach. I don't want him climbing on the furniture and kitchen counters, so I give him something appropriate to climb on. I might buy a Little Tykes slide or put a stack of bed pillows on the floor for him to climb on.

The goal is always to accommodate the developmental need of the toddler without compromising safety and reason. The following scenario took place in the home of someone we know, and illustrates the effects of not understanding a toddler's intention.

Two-year-old Jason was fascinated by the beautiful ornaments on the Christmas tree. He stood in front of the tree gazing at the lights, completely enraptured with its spectacle. He approached the tree, stuck out his finger, and gingerly touched a lovely-but-breakable Christmas ornament. Dad was standing nearby and observed his son's behavior. When he saw the child move toward the tree, he lurched into action, got down on one knee, angrily peered into the child's face, pointed his finger and shouted, "Don't you dare touch that tree. You touch that tree again and you will get a spanking."

A look of terror came across Jason's face, and he recoiled from his father. For a brief moment, it was as if he was frozen in time. When he recovered, he began to cry, frantically looked about for his mother, and ran to her.

So let's think about what just happened. It is clear that the father assumes his son's behavior is willful disobedience. He is touching the Christmas ornament because he chooses to disobey. The father responds in a punitive and shaming manner. The child is left in a state of fear and moves away from the father, seeking comfort from Mom. Dad walks away from this scenario with a ruptured emotional connection between himself and his child.

Let's consider another scenario in a home that is child friendly.

Two-year-old Jason was fascinated by the beautiful ornaments on the Christmas tree. He approached the tree, stuck out his finger, and gingerly touched a lovely-but-breakable Christmas ornament. Dad was standing nearby and observed his son's behavior. When he saw the child move toward the tree, he bent down and said, "They sure are pretty. You like those sparkling red ornaments. But you know what? They can easily break, and the broken glass would hurt you. Let's move this ornament to the top of the tree, and let's put some other non-breakable things down here."

Dad removed a few plastic ornaments from the top and allowed Jason to hang them on the bottom of the tree. Dad put his arm around Jason and they observed the beautiful tree together. Jason's need to explore and touch is met; he is kept safe; and the beauty of the family Christmas tree is preserved. Dad and Jason walk away with their emotional connection strengthened.

Attunement to the Emotional Life of Toddlers

If we're going to form an enduring emotional bond between ourselves and our toddler, it is important that we understand the emotional life of toddlers and what makes them tick. Knowing what's happening within the child allows us "see, hear, and understand" them. Let's begin with a toddler's seemingly favorite word.

A Declaration of Independence

Why do toddlers love the word, "no"?

In the first year of life, there are very few reasons to say "no" to an infant. During infancy, a child's emotional bucket is filled with hundreds and thousands of yes answers. When a baby cries and I feed him in a timely and sensitive manner, I say, yes to the child's needs and I put a yes in his bucket.

When a child cries in discomfort from a soiled diaper and I change the diaper in a timely and sensitive manner, I add another yes to his bucket. The child emerges at the end of the first year with a bucket full of yes answers that contribute to his knowing he is worthy of love and care. He knows his needs are a priority in the family by the consistency and timeliness of the response.

But this quickly changes in toddlerhood. As the child becomes more mobile, the likelihood of "getting into trouble" with Mom and Dad increases and he begins to accumulate a bucket of no answers.

Also at eighteen months, children begin to realize they are a separate individual with their own opinions, preferences, emotions, thoughts, and desires. They're becoming aware of their own inner life. As awareness of their individuality grows, they experiment with this newly discovered realization and "practice" asserting their independence.

The no of a toddler, therefore, is usually a declaration of independence and not the no of rebellion. This is important to understand because if I take it personally and interpret their no as evidence of their rebellious nature, then I am likely to respond with power and control. And likely to be embroiled with my toddler on a daily basis.

I have to find a way to balance their need for independence with their need for structure. That's a tall order for parents. I have a friend who says during this stage of development, parents need to be the "benevolent dictator."

So how do we serve as the "benevolent dictator?" Don't take the no of a toddler personally. Don't engage and try to rationalize with him—you are spitting in the wind. Ignore the no, and give him two choices.

Barbara gives an example: One evening when my granddaughter was two, I walked into the living room just as her dad told her it was time to go to bed. In classic two-year-old form she replied, "No. I not tired."

My son-in-law looked at me and said, "She's yours."

I ignored the no and gave her two yeses by saying, "Would you like a piggy back ride or would you like to walk like a gorilla?"

She immediately responded, "I want a gorilla piggy back ride." She climbed on my back and off to bed we went with no protest.

So what happened here? Ignoring the no and giving two yeses assumes obedience. Going to bed is nonnegotiable; how she gets there is. She can have a piggy back ride or walk like a gorilla, but one way or the other, she is going to bed. In this interaction, I honored her need to assert herself and that's have some control. But at the same time, I communicated an expectation of obedience.

I was in control without being controlling.

Being in control without being controlling is a critical understanding for parents at all stages of development. I always need to be the "boss", but I can do that without being "bossy." What would this scenario have looked like if I responded in a controlling manner? Let's think about it.

"No. I not tired."

I think to myself, I'm going to nip this rebellion in the bud, and respond by saying, "You need to march yourself right up to bed immediately. Do as you are told."

She throws herself on the floor and starts screaming. I pick her up and take her upstairs while she protests, "I don't want to. I'm not tired." I basically have to wrestle with her to get her pajamas on. Her cries get louder and more intense. Soon she is beside herself in a complete emotional meltdown. I have made my point—she is going to bed whether she wants to or not. But she is in a state of emotional disintegration. I have forced compliance and ruptured the connection. I have gained nothing.

Saying No to a Toddler

What do you do when no is the only option? For example, getting buckled into a car seat is nonnegotiable. Inevitably there comes a time when you must go home after a birthday party or an outing at the park. It's always helpful to give toddlers a warning that it is almost time leave. Demanding that they abruptly stop playing and leave is almost certain to evoke some pushback. Even adults like to bring closure to an activity before transitioning to another. Whenever possible, alerting your toddler that you will be leaving soon allows him to know what is coming next instead of being a complete surprise.

Predictability brings a sense of safety.

It is highly likely that, despite your advance warning, you will still get some pushback. Acknowledging your child's desires before kindly but firmly saying no can help buffer some of the distress. For example, I invited a young, single mom and her two-year-old daughter to the house for lunch. We played dolls, picked flowers, and went for a walk. When it came time to go home, she feigned sleepiness and lay on my couch, pretending to snore. Mom told her she could have five more minutes to play and then they would leave.

As soon as Mom said this, the child popped up and went back to playing. After a period of time, Mom once again told the child it was time to leave. She suddenly became very sleepy again and lay down on the couch, pretending to sleep. Mom once again gave her five more minutes to play.

I knew where this was going, so I went over and said, "We have had such a good time today, and I know it is hard to stop playing when you're having fun. But it is time to go home. Let's put the babies to bed." We wrapped up the dolls and put them on the couch to "sleep." Then I took her by the hand and said, "It's time to go to the car."

She balked and said, "No, Miss Barbara."

I picked her up and said, "It is so hard to stop playing when you are having a good time. We played dolls, picked flowers, and took a walk. We had such a good time. But it is time to go home."

As we walked to the car she said over and over, "No, Miss Barbara."

And I kept saying over and over, "I know it is hard to stop playing, but it is time to go home." I buckled her into her seat.

Despite her protests, she compliantly allowed me to buckle her into her seat.

I acknowledged her desire to continue playing before saying no. By picking her up when she resisted going to the car, I communicated to her that I was "big enough" to take care of her. By gently but firmly placing her in the car seat, I communicated that I meant business. This interaction was not harsh or shaming.

By the way, getting buckled into a car seat is often stressful for toddlers. There are many reasons for this. Toddlerhood is a time of exploration and discovery. By nature, toddlers are very active. Riding in a car seat requires a toddler to override their natural tendencies. It also involves a great deal of stimulation to the sensory processing system which, in and of itself, can be stressful. When you consider all of these factors, it is easy to understand why getting buckled in can be so hard. Here are some strategies that may help.

1. Begin telling your child a story as you prepare to go to the car. Build up to a suspenseful ending, and tell your child you will finish the story when he gets buckled in his seat.

2. Give your child a choice as to how he moves to the car: jumping, tiptoeing, stomping, etc.

3. Give your toddler some "deep muscle input." Let them hold something to squeeze.

4. Give your child a snack to eat.

5. Listen to familiar songs. Melodic melodies and rhythm stimulate the safety center of the brain and can help calm your child.

Why Do Toddlers Love the Words, "Me" and "Mine"?

As toddlers become aware of their own preferences, wants, and wishes, they become possessive of their things, and "me" and "mine" become their new favorite words. Another child reaches for their toy, and the toddler starts pushing and screaming, "mine!"

Their inability to share and take turns is the result of a developmental incapacity to take the perspective of another. They are not able to "walk in someone else's shoes" so to speak.

When a toddler walks up to another child and grabs a toy, eliciting a blood-curdling scream, it is a surprise to the toddler. It never occurs to them that someone else also wants the toy. I want the toy and everyone knows that—or so they think.

So the challenge then becomes for parents to attune to the developmental capacities of the toddler while at the same time gently nudging the child into new understandings. Fortunately when it comes to sharing possessions and turn-taking, toddlers are easily distracted.

When your toddler grabs a toy out of the hands of another, you simply give it back to the other child and say something like, "No, that's his. Let's find something for you to play with." You immediately direct the child's attention to something that you know they enjoy. You might roll a beach ball to him. Or you can pick the child up and move the child to a different location and engage his attention in looking out the window, looking at a book, or talking to another adult.

Distraction is a strategy that toddlers respond to much of the time. The key is finding something else that engages their attention, and the previously desired object is quickly forgotten.

We know what you're thinking. But what if my toddler has a meltdown and goes ballistic?

That is likely to happen now and then. First, I acknowledge my toddler's desire. "I know you love to play with that toy." Then, I use some kind of rhythmic touch or rhythmic movement to calm the child. I might pick him up, bounce, rock, or sway gently and talk soothingly. "I know you love playing with the toy he has. When you're ready, we will find a different toy."

Attuning to your toddler means recognizing their developmental incapacities to share and take turns. It means not expecting them to do something they are incapable of doing.

Why Are Toddlers Prone to Meltdowns?

There are many factors that contribute to temper tantrums, but the most common causes are fatigue, hunger, and overstimulation. When you are out in public and see children go into meltdown mode, look at your watch. It's often around mealtime. When blood sugar starts to drop, behavior also deteriorates. When fatigue sets in, even the best of us have trouble behaving well.

Every child has a threshold of too much stimulation. Getting in and out of the car a half-dozen times in a morning and visiting multiple stores can be taxing. Attuned parents are aware of their toddlers' hunger patterns and signals that they are done.

We've all been there—we have a long list of errands that have to get done before that vacation or before the relatives arrive. We get halfway through our agenda, and our toddler loses it. The constant in and out of the car, in and out of a shopping cart, the hustle and bustle take its toll, and we have a screaming toddler on our hands. In these moments, what they need most is to be held, rocked, and soothed.

These kinds of scenes are inevitable and understandable when they happen now and then. But when we consistently ignore our toddler's basic patterns of functioning and overstimulate them on a regular basis, we undermine the emotional connection.

Creating a Play-Based Environment

One of the joys of parenting a toddler is their playfulness. Toddlers initiate many playful experiences that are actually attachment rituals.

They invite Mom and Dad to play chase by looking over their shoulder, giggling and running in the opposite direction. Can you imagine how a toddler would feel if they looked over their shoulder only to see Mom looking at her cell phone instead of chasing? It would not take too many moments of nonengagement before the toddler would give up and never initiate.

Toddlers love hide and seek, Ring around the Rosie, and piggy back rides. They like to "volley" with Mom and Dad by throwing a ball, playing Pat-a-Cake, or Peek-a-Boo. Many start to enjoy rough-and-tumble play with parents and older brothers and sisters.

They may invite you to read with them by plopping a book in your lap. Rocking, cuddling, and snuggling while reading together has profound emotional—as well as cognitive—benefit. The child comes to associate reading with joy and pleasure.

Responding to a toddler's initiations to play is as important as feeding them. Following their lead and accepting their invitation to play in a certain way or with a particular toy is a powerful way a parent demonstrates respect for the child's interests—and reinforces a child's sense of self-efficacy. Playful engagement fills the child's tank with feelings of joy and connection.

If we only play the role of policemen and never the role of playmate, strong emotional connections will be undermined. When we follow children's lead in play, they are more likely to cooperate with us in those moments when compliance is needed. When we hijack children's play and try to divert their attention something we enjoy more, we undermine strong emotional connections.

I (Cathy) was recently observing the interaction between a mom and a toddler. The toddler rolled a beach ball to Mom and eagerly waited for her to return the ball. Mom pushed the ball aside and beckoned the child to sit by her and do a puzzle. The toddler ran to get the ball and threw it toward her. Once again, she ignored his initiation and beckoned him to come sit beside her. He ran off to the other side of the room to play with something else.

Reflections

Watching a toddler explore and discover newfound abilities is perhaps one of the most delightful stages of child development. The enthusiasm of a toddler is contagious and invites you to join in the fun that few can refuse. Coupled with the delight, the toddler begins to learn how to express and exert preferences with boundless energy.

Application

Many of the strategies mentioned in this chapter apply to children of all ages. This week try a couple of them.

1.   Ignore their no and give two yeses from which to choose with enthusiasm.

2.   At a moment of impasse, acknowledge your child's intent or desire before you say no.

3.   Before transitioning to another activity or location, give your child a warning to allow for closure.

4.   Follow the lead of the child in play. Engage in an activity that he clearly enjoys and initiates.

5.   Engage in rough-and-tumble play, if your child clearly indicates that they enjoy it.

6.   Read to your child.

CHAPTER 7

The Interplay of Parent–Child Relationships

By the end of the first year of life, a baby has an identifiable attachment pattern or "template" that tells him what to expect from relationships. When the child receives warm and responsive care from Mom and Dad, he expects to receive the same from childcare providers, extended family, and others with whom he comes in contact. Mom and Dad meet his needs for intimacy in a warm and consistent manner. His needs are met by those whose voice, smell, and touch are familiar. This has served to relay the beginnings of a primary relationship with his mother.

If the needs of his mother have been met during her pregnancy and she has maintained a stable emotional life, the child will be the beneficiary of the same experience. He will comfortably transition from the warmth of the womb to the new and expanded environment of a home life with additional sights, sounds, and stimulation.

In contrast, if his mother has been exposed to a harsh and unpredictable pregnancy, with little support or resources to nurture his intrauterine development, he will transition into the world with the experience and expectation of negative interactions. It will be difficult for this child to enjoy a state of calmness and sense of well-being due to the adverse impact on his regulatory system.

A child who is adopted or fostered at birth has suffered a rupture of the biological bond. It is experienced as a loss of all that is familiar. It is important to recognize this truth and provide intense and intentional focus on nurture and security. This initial loss is significant and requires a greater degree of felt safety, availability, sensory communication, playful engagement, and attunement.

As the needs of the infant become more directly experienced by the mother and father, care becomes increasingly demanding. If the parents are well resourced with preparation, education, and support and have created an environment of emotional and physical stability, the child will develop a sense of security and healthy attachment. On the other hand, a child born into an inconsistent, unpredictable, and unprepared home environment will be insecure in his approach to the world and fail to develop secure attachment relationships.

Parents who are ill-equipped to meet the dependency needs of children are likely to be overwhelmed with the 24/7 demands of infants who are unable to care for themselves. When parents expect babies to immediately reciprocate their love and affection, they may become disillusioned and disappointed with their infants. This sets the stage for unrealistic expectations, which can lead to unhealthy attachment patterns. The danger is we unconsciously absorb our parents' feelings and attitudes toward us and carry those feelings around for the rest of our lives.

Seventy percent of us will maintain the same attachment pattern we had at one year of age and reproduce that same pattern with our own children. Our initial parent child interactions affect our approach to all future relationships. The type of attachment relationship we experience has a ripple effect on all aspects of development and across future generations. This is why healthy attachment is so critical.

There are four types of attachment patterns, and each describes a different kind of attachment that characterizes the parent–child relationship.

1. Secure Attachment

Secure attachment is fostered by a parent who maintains emotional balance and provides for their infant a calm and stable environment that prepares them for the challenges of the world beyond the home. Attuned parents accurately read the sensory cues of the infant and respond in a way that makes sense to the child. For example, a child turns his head away when mom is attempting to give him a spoonful of applesauce. But Mom insists that the baby needs to eat it all. She continues to prod and poke until the baby finally screams in protest. Consequently, mealtimes were inevitably unpleasant. On the other hand, Mom recognizes the turning of the head as the baby's way of saying they have had enough. She respects the child's cues, follows his lead, and doesn't try to cajole, bribe, or force the baby to eat more. The attuned mom and baby are able to enter into a reciprocal dance of nonverbal communication and respect for one another's needs.

Nurturing parents can adapt to increasing demands of the infant because they have structured their lives to make this experience a priority. Securely attached children typically have attuned parents who have a reasonable degree of emotional strength and maturity. They limit their obligations, conserve their energies and efforts to provide the infant with consistency of food, attention, and availability. The parents respond quickly and warmly to the child's distress and basic needs with a gentle touch and soothing voice. This communicates to the infant a sense of security and comfort that allows the infant to truly rest without undue attention to outside stimulation.

When an infant experiences the full attention of their parent and bathes in all the sensory delights of sight, sound, and movement, he begins to function within the comfort of consistency, stability, and predictability. Even though parenting an infant is a demanding task, these parents find great pleasure and joy in meeting the needs of their child. Playful interactions become a normal and regular part of the relationship, and mutual delight between parent and child is obvious.

The child has developed a "secure base" of trust that then allows the child to feel safe to explore as he makes his way through the developmental tasks of infancy. Exploration is the flip side of attachment. Using his parents as a secure base, the toddler ventures out, stopping to look back or return to be refueled for the next foray away from his nurturing parent. As soon as he has wandered too far, has experienced fear, or has been startled, he quickly returns to the safe haven of his parent, seeking physical closeness. This safety, exploration, and seeking of physical proximity to an available attachment figure are the hallmarks of secure attachment.

Children with secure attachments approach the world with an overall sense of hope and curiosity. They are pleasant to be around and have an internal sense that they are enjoyable and worthy of care. They get along with other children, respond well to appropriate adult authority, accept comfort from others when hurt or upset, and enjoy exploring the world and trying new things.

When they enter school, their energies can be invested in learning rather than merely coping, because they have an inner sense of security and belief that the world is a safe place.

That isn't to say securely attached children don't have their moments—they do. But they quickly recover from momentary discord and get back on track to enjoy life and relationships. They trust others will act in their best interest. The security afforded a child who is securely attached paves the road for future pursuits, as these children aren't preoccupied with having to attend to factors outside themselves, either from sensory distractions or relational distress.

If an older child is not demonstrating attachment security, it is important to meet them at the developmental stage in which they are functioning. Attention to building sensory comforts through holding, rocking, eye contact, and the building blocks of earlier attachment need to be tended to meet those former dependency needs.

The next two styles of attachment focus on insecurity expressed in two ways: preoccupied or anxious parenting and ambivalent or avoidant parenting.

2. Insecure Anxious and Ambivalent Attachment

When parents haven't received warm, loving attention as infants, it is sometimes hard to know what emotional support to give to their child.

In looking back at how you were parented, it is important to understand your personal history, in view of: your parents' availability, having your feelings respected, and means of comfort given you by touch, sight, and sound. Were your parents available to you or involved in other pursuits such that you were to be "seen but not heard"? Were they able to provide encouraging words and sensitive touch when you were in need?

It is important to understand that those who parent from an insecure position are not bad people. They're typically people who are overwhelmed by life and simply don't have the resources to cope. They genuinely love their kids, but they don't have the emotional resources to provide consistent nurture and care. They are often overwhelmed by finances, health issues, or other life stressors. They have the best of intentions but are unable to provide the consistency of care required by babies and young children.

Parents with an anxious and ambivalent attachment style tend to be unsure of how to parent, and instead of being a calming source of balance and equilibrium for a baby's upset, they tend to absorb the baby's anxiety. This parent may become stressed and rattled to the point that they are unable to deliver comfort and meet the infant's needs.

Insecure parenting is observed in those who are preoccupied to the point that they are unable to reliably respond to their children. Parents may show a lack of interest because they are so involved in their own lives they may miss vital cues to attune to their child's needs. They may be thinking of other things—a business meeting, obligation, or activity—instead of focusing their attention on the here and now. They are unable to accurately see, hear, and understand their child in the moment. As a result, they will be unable to read their child's needs.

For example, a five-year-old girl in Daddy's arms tries to get her father's attention while he's looking at his cell phone. Dad doesn't notice his daughter's bid for attention until his child physically pulls his chin toward her in order to get him to look into her eyes.

These parents may be so preoccupied that they fail to notice instances when their child needs their protection, yet be over-protective and impose limits that are inappropriate based on the child's need. A lack of attunement can result in the parent sending mixed messages that are confusing to the child.

Preoccupied parents are out of sync with their children's needs and are likely to impose their own interpretation of a particular situation and respond out of their own needs rather than to the need of the child.

Another common example: Mom lets her young child repeatedly run down a steep hill with no supervision but doesn't let her child play on the age-appropriate playground equipment because she is on the phone with a friend.

The neediness of the parent can sometimes result in a role reversal whereby the parent expects the child to meet the parent's emotional needs. The child is expected to provide reassurance and support to the anxious adult.

This reversal of roles leaves the child feeling unprotected and unsure of how to fulfill Mom's expectations and needs. For example, a four-year-old becomes Mom's confidant in regard to a messy divorce situation. Mom has no friends and expects her child to fill this void. The child bears emotional and psychological burdens she is unprepared to carry.

The unpredictable behavior of the ambivalent parents sets up unreliable protection for the child, leaving him feeling anxious in response. Sometimes the parent responds quickly with warmth and affection and, at other times, with anger and irritability. Or, they may not respond at all.

The uncertainty of response can lead to the child using exaggerated emotion to manipulate parents to get what they want. Feelings are often exaggerated because they're never quite certain parents will take note of their distress, and intense emotions are certain to get the parent's attention. As children get older, they may resort to temper tantrums or attention-seeking behaviors.

Children with insecure anxious attachment can be both demanding and clingy. They are difficult to satisfy—nothing is ever quite right. In times of conflict, they may escalate the situation to maintain control and keep the attention of the adult.

The small child hits his head on the table and while he's crying, Mommy frantically says, "Tell me you're okay, tell me you're okay!"

The four year-old is left to get his own breakfast.

The request for school supplies by the third grader is ignored for days while the child suffers the embarrassment of not being prepared for school.

Children who have been insecurely and anxiously parented struggle in relationships with others. They are uncomfortable with intimacy and closeness and give the impression they can take care of themselves. They live life in their heads rather than being connected with others at an emotional level.

The six-year-old playing with a friend keeps wondering when Mommy is coming back. His friend keeps trying to get him to focus on the trucks they are playing with, but the six-year-old fears being abandoned, is unable to give attention to playing with his friend, and worries, When will she be back? Will she leave me here?

The insecure ambivalent child struggles to fully engage with his peers. He is so preoccupied and anxious that he is unable to enjoy relationships with others. His need to control the attention of adults leaves him unable to relax and fully participate in play. He constantly gets interrupted by his lack of being able to focus on his connection with another. He is unsure of what will come next, is unable to read the cues of his friend, and vacillates between feeling anxious and angry. His response is unfocused and nervous, due to his feelings of anxiety and emotional uncertainty.

This is the result of the child whose parents have not been attuned to his needs for comfort and fear. They are often parents who want to avoid the anxiety of separations and leave the child without warning or the memory of an affectionate goodbye. They sneak out under the pretense of not wanting to upset the child, but the real concern is their own angst or wanting to hurry up and get on with their day.

Research indicates some other interesting tendencies as well.

Insecure, anxious children are more likely to become addicted to substances later in life than children with other forms of attachment are, and they're more likely to become victims of bullying behavior. Insecure in their relationships with others, they self-medicate to ease their lack of social skills and often let others take advantage of them, unsure of how to navigate secure relationships of give-and-take.

Anxiously attached babies cry more at one year of age than other children and can be difficult to soothe. As babies, their "voice" was often ignored, so they resort to other forms of manipulation to get what they want.

CHAPTER 8
Insecure, Dismissive, and Avoidant Attachment

The parent who displays an avoidant or dismissive style of attachment is likely to be a parent who demands compliance from, and exerts control and authority over, a child. They may be somewhat rigid and require unreasonably high expectations of their children. Focused on their own standards of acceptable emotion and behavior, they tend to be unable or unwilling to accept the cues the young child exhibits.

For example, a mother ends her seven-year-old's play date abruptly and without warning. She demands, "Pick up these toys and clean up this room. We've got to go now!" By dismissing her son's need for closure, her interaction is likely to evoke an aggressive protest from her child.

Her dismissive response gives the child no advance warning that soon they must leave, and prevents him from bringing some positive closure to a fun time had with a friend. Avoidant parents exhibit no attunement to the child's need end an activity with a sense of positive feeling and successful social skill mastery.

These parents may read their child's needy behavior as manipulative or not to be tolerated. They desire for their children to be and act more "grown up," thinking their world to be silly and something to be rapidly "grown past." Insecure/dismissed children are typically raised in homes where the interaction between parent and child is characterized by harshness and irritability. The neediness of their children overwhelms the parent, and they respond with anger and frustration. Sometimes these parents are dealing with mental illness, addiction, or clinical depression. Catastrophic illness or injury, poverty, or other trauma may also be the source of overwhelming stress.

The dismissive parent may be a single mom who is struggling to survive emotionally and financially—or a father who's trying to deal with a mentally ill wife and two small children. These parents rarely if ever have a support system to encourage them in life's struggles.

Dismissive and avoidant parents may fail to protect their children and allow them to take unnecessary risks. This reinforces their views that growth is achieved through action, regardless of readiness. They view themselves as tough in their parenting and compliance is valued as positive, with little regard to their child's "voice." They don't take the time to nurture their child with encouragement or teach skills progressively, building skill development at the child's pace. Instead, they issue commands to be followed.

Children parented by dismissive and avoidant parents may develop two types of avoidant behavior: "aggressive avoidant" or "withdrawn avoidant."

The "aggressively avoidant" child views intimacy as a threat, and they respond with anger and pushback. At times, these children may seem to take delight in the discomfort or pain of others. This may be the child who avoids eye contact, who may find more pleasure in things rather than people, and who rarely seeks out comfort from others when they're hurt. They can be sullen, oppositional, and ignore requests from parents.

They're unable to express empathy toward others because they haven't experienced empathetic care.

Johnny is a preschooler who belittles his playmates. He is always the last to line up on the playground, ignoring the reminders from his teachers. With other children, he brags about being the best at activities and points out the inabilities of other children to complete activities as well as he can. He makes fun of their artwork. Avoidant children mask their insecurity with bravado and an inflated view of self at the expense of others.

The "withdrawn avoidant" child tries to fly below the radar and be perfect so as not to draw attention to himself. He has learned that attention may elicit an angry or harsh response; to avoid these uncomfortable interactions, he withdraws and isolates himself. Often, these children are regarded as "perfect" children because they require so little time and attention from parents and caregivers.

Both the aggressive avoidant and the withdrawn avoidant are Lone Rangers, and their journey through life is often characterized by alienation, isolation, and self-protection.

Research indicates that by the time these children are in middle to late elementary school, they can become the school bullies. They have little empathy for others because their parents were unable to show them empathetic care.

The avoidant child can be prone to sudden and violent emotional outbursts. Outwardly, they may seem cool, calm, and collected most of the time, but strong emotions simmer below the surface. A seemingly small incident may trigger a violent or extreme response.

Insecurely dismissive and avoidant children are typically raised in homes where the interaction between parent and child is characterized by harshness and irritability.

There is yet another dynamic in the homes of our modern culture that creates avoidant relationships. That dynamic involves materialism that can masquerade as success.

Mom and Dad are on the fast track to high-powered careers. They bring children into the mix simply because it's the expected thing to do. Nurturing their children is inconvenient and gets in the way of their lifestyle and their career. They gladly pay others to care for their children and meet their needs. The neediness of their kids is a source of irritation.

Outwardly, these children appear to have everything they need: designer clothes, every toy and gadget on the market. They are provided lessons in everything from tennis to voice to piano and martial arts. They attend the best private schools, but these children are often lacking genuine warmth and connection to their parents.

It's a sad indictment on our current society.

There's a Chinese proverb that says, "The best time to plant a tree is twenty years ago. But the next best time to plant a tree is today." You may be seeing aspects of your parenting that could foster insecure or avoidant behavior. But you can still apply what you're learning from this book with your children.

It may take more grace, patience, and determination the older your child becomes, but never stop nurturing your child.

Put down your smartphone, and turn off the TV. Begin to see who your child is and what their needs might be at that moment. Honestly assess your own style of attachment and attune yourself to your child in an unhurried way. Provide your child with the security, nurturing, and soft words of encouragement they crave. Have regular fun together; get out the toys, and make a habit of family game nights!

Reactive Attachment Disorder

Children diagnosed with severe attachment disorders typically suffer from extreme abuse and neglect early in life. Attachment occurs on a continuum from a child being securely attached in relationship to their parents, to severely disordered—not able to form or consistently maintain security in relationships.

Children who have been parented at the extreme end of a disorganized attachment style are in the greatest need. This can prevent them from forming trust with another human being. These children are often diagnosed with Reactive Attachment Disorder, typically suffering chronic and extreme abuse or deprivation early in life. Extreme abuse can be overwhelmingly detrimental to the mind, body, and soul, and as debilitating as any chronic disease. Abuse can change us physiologically as well as emotionally.

Too often, these children have no feelings of hope, no sense of self-worth, or no comprehension of human affection. Sometimes children with Reactive Attachment Disorder are adopted into loving, well-adjusted families, but their adoptive parents soon realize love is not enough. Parenting a child with extreme attachment disorder requires specialized knowledge, training, and commitment.

Research by Purvis and Cross has demonstrated that healing can and does happen, and there is enormous reason for hope.

They note the ingredients in healing children with complex trauma. They include the following:

- Empowering the child by providing a foundation of safety in their lives
- Connection to healing and secure relationships
- Correction of ineffective behavior patterns and development of effective coping and self-regulating behavior

Parents of children with attachment disorders need an understanding of attachment, a neurological perspective of brain development under stress, extreme patience, and access to resources. These, along with heightened self-care and accessible support systems, will help to effectively parent.

While this can be daunting, for parents who make parenting children with complex trauma their priority, there is hope. Remember that a struggling child's expressions of anger or pain are not based on an opposition toward you. Their behavior is how they've learned to protect themselves. Through the availability of a loving parent, broken trust can be slowly, methodically, and lovingly rebuilt.

Reflections

What can I do on a practical level to foster secure attachments?

Children are both a gift and responsibility. The first three years of a child's life set the stage for their sense of security. Make knowing your child's temperament, their individual cues about needs, and your response a priority.

Mindfulness, in this context, means being aware of yourself, your emotions, attitude, and behavior in relation to the developing and changing needs of your child. This is an active process of reminding yourself to be observant, in an unhurried manner, of the cues being given by your child.

Be emotionally available to your child. Put away work, put down phones, step away from the computer, and greatly limit TV time, so you can learn about your child's unique personality and cues on how to promote connection in your relationship.

Connect sensory comforts with soothing words. Gently touch and use rhythmic movement and focused eye contact. Provide food in an unhurried way—let a child "digest" and observe who you are on many nonverbal levels: smiles, animated faces, rocking, and massage.

Move with your child at a slow pace that meets the need for transitions to unfold at a manageable rate. Our society has fostered a quick pace of rushed schedules and endless obligations. Plan ahead for changes throughout the day to ensure a relaxed pace. Pack bags for tomorrow's outing tonight, think ahead in planning menus, clothes, and what is needed to make transitions easier.

When you come together before or after a period of separation (upon awakening, return from work/school, and before bed) nurture yourself and your child with lap time and intentional relaxation to promote attunement. Feel the co-regulation of shared heart rate that occurs when you enjoy this level of unhurried physical contact.

Realize that relationships are connections that can be changed by positive actions and attitude. Every day presents new opportunities.

CHAPTER 9

Creating a Higher Sense of Intimacy with Your Partner

The next skill that we need to look at is how you can create more intimacy with your partner. There are a lot of different ways that you can create this intimacy and being able to create it and maintain it will make a world of difference in how strong your relationship is.

Now, when we are talking about intimacy here, we need to understand that we are not talking just about sex. While sex is an important part of a healthy relationship, and should be something that you can discuss comfortably, and consider with your partner on a regular basis as your sexual desires and needs change over time, it is important to remember that there are other forms of intimacy that need to be focused on in order to help your relationship grow stronger and your relationship to stay around.

By the way, it's important that we speak to a large extent on sexual communication, how it helps to build your relationship and avoid insincerity from any party. Partners in a relationship who fail to bring up matters on sex may be due to them seeing it as a lesser topic for deliberation, or it doesn't seem pleasant to them, is at a risk of some kind. It is important to question your partner of your lapses and where you've to make amends. It shouldn't piss you off or cause a disagreement. It is a route to building a reliable and lasting relationship.

Sexual communication is expected to be at the peak of topics for discussion in every relationship that aims to grow stronger and longer. This creates a balancing ground for partners and shaves off distrust of any kind. It is no doubt that a huge number of persons find it absurd or, less important to discuss sex with their partners whenever they feel sober or unsatisfied. They feel the best is to consult a third party, whether through books, findings made through the internet or their friends or relatives, they find comfort from this discussion and sought remedies, this is done with the total exclusion and awareness of their partner.

Why should there even be a sexual communication in the first place? Sexual communication is so cogent that it must not be sidelined in any relationship. It has a way of building the sensation that creates a strong bond, it makes partners share the innermost part of themselves which invariably makes them share other parts of themselves, intrinsic or extrinsic troubles. You should not be ashamed of letting your partner know where he needs to make amend. "Oh, the styles are cool, do make a readjustment here", the mode at which this discussion should be made must be on a polite and frank note, you can do the jokes but with a sincere face, let them know their what bothers pertaining their sexual activities.

Therefore, how then do we make this sexual communication on a simple note, concise, conservative and with honesty. The steps are as follows:

1. Do not bring up this topic after having sex: You know that moment when the truth hurts, when it might not be so easy to bear, that is the period. You should not bring up matters related to the sex you made abruptly, it demeans your partner sense of humor and it could result into a misunderstanding.

When is suitable to bring up the matter for ironing? It could come later during your bedtime or when there's an outing involving just the two of you but not immediately after the sex.

2. Do not make your conversation on sex seem like a shock to the partner: This is very much important, there are times to convey your message and it will be swiftly understood. You should try to present these matters in a happy atmosphere. You should endeavor not to speak the truth that may destabilize your partner when you unleash his shortfalls. The conversation that has deepened the interest of your partner is an open space to let them know. It'll make them know of the need to fill the loopholes and connect those pleasures you want to feel during your sexual intercourse.

3. A quiet place far from home: There is a possible case of not having a quiet time with your partner. Tight work schedule, children frolicking, and the chores at home gives you no time for your partner. Make a quiet time. Maybe somewhere far from home where the children are far from earshot. This quiet place is an opportunity for both partners to reminisce on their sexual life. You can talk on when you both first had sex, this will then extend into discussing your present situation. Do you feel the warmth as much as you felt during your first night? Do you feel that absolute pleasure during sex or has it deflated? Do you feel that wondrous sensation that looks unquenchable or it has started to fade? These and many more are what you can talk on during this quiet time.

4. Present it in the form of a suggestion: The erratic behavior of people to when sexual discourse is brought for discussion that nails them to a fault makes it so difficult for partners to anger their beloved. This is why you must present it in the

form of a suggestion. This won't all the time sound embarrassing or seen as a means to belittle him. Your choice of words must be cautiously chosen so as not to arouse their anger.

If you adhere to the enlisted ways, it will help you enormously in bringing up sexual matters with your partner. If you feel you are enclosed in thoughts pertaining to your sex life because you're trying to maintain the relationship, the harbored thoughts will further lessen your strength and leave you in shatters. Therefore, ponder on every word herein, muster that heart to bring up matters of your sexual life with your relationship and you shall have more than one cause to enjoy a lasting relationship. To reiterate, relationship that sidelines sexual communication is open to seismic disruption. Love them but most importantly talk about your sexual life with your partner.

How do you control your partner if they react badly?

Sexual communication should not sprout any bit of quarrel, but it should rather be a basis to build a comforting relationship lay on honesty, understanding, openness, and love. The above phase that talked on when and the appropriate time and place to bring up matters that relate to your sexual life with you partner will also tremendously help us in treating reaction too. For example, the quiet place that was proposed, if they react disorderly, you are in the position to put them in order. Make them know the importance of your sexual life and why they need to give ears to your suggestion.

Sex can't be completely separated from a relationship and a relationship that never bothers on the pleasure derived by the partners is most likely not last long. You must be able to bring joy to yourself if you can face your partner and let them know the importance of sex in modifying the mightiness of your union.

In building your intimacy through other means, to start with, we are going to talk about the five steps that you need to follow in order to create some more emotional intimacy with your partner. Emotional intimacy allows you and your partner a way to not only look good on paper, and to the outside world, but also to look good on the inside. It allows you both to know each other deeply, in a way that no one else should know you or your partner.

The good news is that this intimacy can be obtainable, no matter how long you have been in the relationship. As long as both of you are willing to invest the time being vulnerable, and you are willing to talk to each other, you can make this work. Some of the steps that you can follow to create a deeper sense of intimacy between you and your partner includes:

When you start the conversation, pick out safer topics

When you first get started, you don't want to just jump into the tough stuff. Even if you have been into the relationship for a long time, jumping into the deep stuff can be intimidating, and can make one or both of you feel nervous and unsure of how you should proceed. Starting with some of the safer topics, the ones that you are both pretty sure how the other one is going to respond can be a much better option. This allows you to feel more comfortable, to get the hang of the process, and can build up some confidence for when you get deeper into this process.

So, to start, you need to focus your conversation. You can choose to do this for a few months or any length of time that you would like. Make sure that you set aside a good 30 minutes a day to talk and work on this. And when you start, you want to make sure that you are working with some comfortable topics so that this activity is more enjoyable, and you will be more willing to stick with it for the long term.

There are a lot of different questions that you can talk to your partner about with this in mind. You can ask them about some of the memories that they remember back from when you were dating and ask why that memory is so important to them. Ask if there is something that they would love to be able to go back and do again.

Make it clear that both partners can share anything

When you are working on these conversations, make sure that both parties know that anything is safe to say or share during this time. Starting out with these conversations can be hard, but when everyone knows that they are in a safe space then they may be more willing to go along with it. You and your partner both want what is best for one another, so why try to make the other one feels bad or feels worried about what is going on when they tell you something?

This isn't an excuse for one or the other to be mean to each other. You can't go into this and say all of the bad things that your partner has ever done wrong in the relationship. This isn't going to be productive, and can make it almost impossible for them to feel good or open up to you. This is supposed to be a time for the two of you to learn more about each other, and to gain a fuller knowledge about one another. If one of the partners feels like they are being attacked, then they aren't going to open up, and they will probably try to get out of doing this again.

The point here is for the conversation to be a good way for you and your partner to become vulnerable with each other. This is the only way that the two of you are going to become more intimate with each other in this sense of the word. If you aren't opening up the floor as a safe space, then it is going to be almost impossible to get any further.

Learn what is going to make your partner come alive

The next thing that we need to take a look at is figuring out what makes your partner come alive. You may need to ask some questions to figure this out, and you will really need to listen in order to hear it. But if you are willing to really pay attention to your partner (and you are with them because you really love and care about them), you will be able to get those results in no time.

For example, maybe you start talking to your partner and say something like "will you explain to me why you like the herbs and flowers so much?" This can get your partner up and running with all of the details, and you may notice that they get more animated and start lighting up at the eyes and with a smile. If you ask a question like this, and start getting that positive response, then take the time to listen to what your partner is telling you.

Now, this doesn't mean that you are going to fully understand what they are saying, and maybe the whole thing seems a bit boring to you. If the man goes on and on about cars, you may have no interest in it at all. If the woman talks about flowers and gardening during this time, it is likely that you will want to kind of close it all out. But in reality, you have to be willing to listen and hear what the other person is saying.

This is going to go a long way in developing some of the intimacy that you are looking for in your relationship. It doesn't matter what your feelings on the matter are, or even if you really understand what your partner is saying in the process. What matters is that you are actually learning about the things that are important to your partner, the things that make them excited and bring them alive.

If you hear the section above and you aren't able to answer the question about what brings your partner out and makes them feel alive, then it is time to make some changes and have that conversation with them. It can be a really simple question that starts it off and gets you going. But you may have to dig around a bit to find it.

Time to bring out the tough questions

After you have had some time to follow some of the tips that we discussed above, it is time to take this to the next level. At some point, you will need to start introducing some of the harder questions to the mix. This isn't meant to be a challenge to you, or even to scare you at all. But how are you supposed to develop a better level of intimacy with your partner if you aren't willing to stop and ask some of these questions along the way.

You will find that most of the healing, as well as the bonding, in your relationship is going to come when you are willing to take on some of the more difficult topics and ask the tough questions. There are a lot of different questions that you can ask when it comes to this, but remember that you are in a safe space, and you are sharing with someone who has agreed to spend the rest of their life with you, and who loves you.

There are a lot of questions that you need to ask your partner. You can ask questions like what makes you feel fearful, what has hurt you, what are the words that tend to crush your heart and do I say them sometimes? You can start out with these and move on to some that are a bit deeper and correspond with the direction that the conversation goes after you ask the questions.

As you ask these questions, make sure that you provide your uninterrupted attention to your partner, and that they do the same for you when it is your time. This is not the time to offer suggestions to the other person, to criticize your partner, or even to inject your own stories. This is the time for you to really learn more about your partner and the things that are important to them, the things that affect them, and the things that you both need to work on together.

If you are trying to come up with some questions that could be used during this phase, think about some of the questions that may be difficult for your partner to answer, but if they did take the time to answer, and you took the time to really listen to the answers that you are given, could help to lead you both to a deeper level of emotional connection. These are the questions that need to be asked during this time.

Of course, you need to spread these out a bit. You probably don't have hours upon hours to spend on these questions in one day. And if all of your sessions become about these, they can get emotional, hard to work with, and can drain you out of energy. Maybe start out your session with a few jokes, some shared memories, and a bit of the easier questions, and then, toward the end of the discussion, go into some of these deeper questions, and then slowly work on those. Remember that you are the one in charge of the conversation, so you can decide what happens when.

Remember to invite God into these conversations all the time

While the conversation is physically happening with you and your partner, it is still a good idea for you to add God into it as well. You will find that by simply adding God, and inviting Him, into your conversations, will be life-changing. There are going to be times when you and your partner are talking, and you notice that there are behaviors and some negatives attitudes that keep coming back over and over again. These could even be some that you and your partner talked about a few times and felt like you were actually healing a bit.

When these happen, it may be time to pray to God about these, and to figure out what you are really feeling. For example, you may identify the emotion as a form of anger. But as you pray to God and invite Him into the conversation, you may start to notice that instead of that emotion being anger, it is actually that you are feeling like your partner is not appreciating you. From there, you can ask when you started to feel that way. Keep in mind that this could bring out some painful incidents in your mind, but give that pain to God, and ask Him what you should do with this pain.

Basically, once you invite God into your conversations and into the relationship, it is going to help clear up the path that you are on with your partner. As humans, there are going to be times when you get stuck, when you look at things in the wrong way, or you just won't know how you should act in order to make sure that you are getting things done and fixed. And that is fine. But when you start to add God into the conversation and start asking Him to give you help and guidance, you will be amazed at the changes that are going to start appearing in your life and in to your relationship.

Your relationship with God is going to be directly related to the relationship and the union that you have with your partner. When you are able to add in some more emotional intimacy and depth to your relationship with God, this is going to translate into receiving the same things in your relationship.

Simple connection exercises to help build intimacy

In the exercises above, we talked mostly about the conversation that you can have with your partner in order to create some of this intimacy. We also took some time to explore how adding God into the conversation, and into your relationship, can make a big difference as well. Now we are going to take a closer look at a few connection exercises that you can add to this that can-do wonders for building up some more intimacy with your partner.

The weekly CEO meeting

Sometimes, it is hard to connect with your partner because you both have to deal with really busy lives. And when you are running around all of the time, trying to keep up with your work, your appointments and so much more. And with all of this craziness is going to contain a lot of errors in communication that will occur through the course of a week including unheard desires, unmet expectations, and unfinished arguments.

Let's think of this method like the weekly CEO meeting, and as a way to take out all of your unfinished business and then hold it up to the light at the end of the work. So, to make sure that this exercise happens, you and your partner need to take some time to schedule a non-negotiable 30-minute connection block each week, or more than once a week if needed, in order to meet up with your partner. Make sure that you both remove all of the distractions from the environment, including your children, the computers, phones, and so on, and sit down and have a conversation like the grownups that you both are.

If you were scheduled to have a meeting with the CEO of your company, how important would you make this meeting? Would you keep rescheduling it, or bring your children to the meeting, or use your phone all of the time so that you don't hear what the CEO says about you? Then why would you do it during this CEO meeting with your partner?

Yes, things are going to get busy. And sometimes it is hard to find the babysitter or to turn off the phone when you are waiting for something that is important to come through. Your relationship should be one of the most important things to you at all times. And you shouldn't let other things get in the way and make it difficult. These meetings are very important, and they are so needed to maintain the open communication and intimacy that you need with your partner. Don't put them off, and don't let other things come between the two of you and interrupt the time that you have.

When you have these meetings, they don't have to be super informal. Just make sure that you are ready to spend this uninterrupted time away from others so that you can just focus on many miscommunications that come up between the two of you during the week.

5 things...Go!

This is something that can be a lot of fun and it is quick and simple. This makes it easier for you to use, even if you are dealing with kids and are too busy to get it all done for that day. For this one, you and your partner both need to come up with a unique theme or code word. You can come up with a different one each time that you do this, or just have one that you are able to bring up any time it is needed.

Whenever your partner calls out that unique code word or theme that you picked out, then you both need to go through with 4 things within that certain topic. For example, you could have our theme be 5 things that you are grateful about in life, five things that you love about your partner, or five things that you would love to do with your partner within the next few weeks.

With this one, you can either both take turns counting out the five, or you can each alternate your turns to make sure that you are both getting the chance. The fact that this exercise is really playful and versatile makes it a winner for most couples. You are allowed to get as creative as you want with this, and you are surely going to be able to come up with a good list that works for everyone. The only limitations that come with this are your own imagination.

CHAPTER 10

Tips for Improving Communication Between Couples

No one is an impeccable communicator. Yet, you can work to improve as a communicator by attempting a couple of the things mentioned in this chapter. All of them may not work for you, nor will they work on all occasions. Better communication, nonetheless, begins with one person endeavoring to enhance, which frequently urges the other to tag along.

Keep Physical Intimacy Alive

Human presence is actualized by touch. You can take the example of a newborn child to realize the vitality of a casual, cherishing touch and the effect on your mental and overall health. These profits don't end in adolescence. An existence without physically being in touch with others is a desolate life for sure.

Studies have indicated that a loving touch really helps the body's levels of oxytocin, a hormone that impacts holding and connection. In a relationship between two grown-up partners, physical intimacy is frequently the foundation of a healthy bond. On the other hand, sexual intimacy should not be the only reason for physical closeness between two people. Consistent, tender touch—holding hands, embracing, or kissing—is just as critical.

Be sensitive towards your partner's likings and desires. While touch is a fundamental part of a sound relationship, it is critical to comprehend the likes and dislikes of your partner in this regard as well. Unwanted touching or unseemly suggestions can make the other individual worry and retreat, which is precisely what you don't need.

Here are some basic approaches to associate as a couple and rekindle love:

- Commit to getting to know one another all the time

Throughout extremely occupied and distressing times, a couple of minutes of truly communicating and associating can help keep bonds solid.

- Find something that you appreciate doing together, whether it is a pastime, a walk, or a talk over some tea or coffee in the morning.

- Try something new together

Doing new things together can be a fun approach to unite and keep things intriguing. It can be as straightforward as attempting another restaurant or going on a day trek to a spot you've never been to previously.

Couples are regularly more fun and fun-loving in the early phases of a relationship. Be that as it may, this perky state of mind can, in some cases, be overlooked as life difficulties or old feelings of disdain begin to act as a burden. Keeping a comical inclination can really help you get through intense times, diminish stress, and work through issues all the more effectively.

Concentrate On Having a Fabulous Time Together

- Think about fun-loving approaches to astound your partner, such as bringing a bunch of flowers or a most loved film home as a surprise.

- Learn from the "play masters" together. Playing with pets or little kids can truly help you reconnect with your perky side. On the off chance that it is something you do together, you likewise get to know more about your partner, and how he or she jumps at the chance to have fun.

- Make a propensity of laughing together whenever you can. Most circumstances are not as dreary as they appear if you add a bit of humor to your approach.

Figuring Out How to Play Once More

A little cleverness and fun-loving collaboration can go far in calming strained circumstances and helping you see the brighter side. In case you're feeling somewhat corroded, take in more about how fun-loving communication can enhance your relationship.

Question Your Presumptions

In the event that you've known one another for some time, you may expect that your partner has a really great idea of what you are thinking and what you require. However, your partner is not a mind reader. While your partner may have some clue, it is much healthier to specifically express your needs. Your partner may sense something, yet it may not be what you require. Also, individuals change, and what you required and needed five years back, for instance, may be altogether different from what the case is now. Getting in the habit of communicating your needs helps you withstand troublesome times, which otherwise may lead to expansion of hatred, misconstruing, and outrage.

Use Your Senses

The most ideal approach to lessen stressful issues rapidly and dependably is through your senses. At the same time, each individual reacts diversely to stress, so you have to discover things that are mitigating to you.

Healthy Associations Are Based On Give-and-Take

If you are hoping to get a 100% return on what you have given in, then you can expect to get disappointed and frustrated in the long run. A healthy relationship is nothing less than a balanced trade off, and each individual needs to play a part to verify that there is a sensible trade.

Don't Make "Winning" Your Objective

On the off chance that you approach your partner with the demeanor that things must be as per your direction, it will be hard to achieve a trade-off. Once in a while this disposition hails from not having your needs met while you were a child, or it could be from years of collected disdain developing in your current relationship. It's okay to have solid feelings about something. However, your partner should be heard, too. You are more likely to get your needs met if you regard what your partner needs, and trade off when you can.

Figure Out How to Deferentially Manage Clash

Clash is certain in any relationship, yet to keep a relationship solid, both individuals need to feel they've been listened to. The objective is not to win, but to solve the clash with deference and affection.

- Communicate that you are reasonable and open for discussion.

- Don't assault somebody specifically; utilize "I" statements to convey how you feel.

- Don't drag old contentions into the mix.

- Keep your focus on the issue close by, and regard the other individual's feelings just as much.

Don't take out your frustration on your partner. Life hassles can make us touchy. In the event that you are adapting to a considerable measure of anxiety, it may appear simpler to snap at your partner. Battling like this may at first feel like a discharge, yet it gradually harms your relationship. Discover different approaches to vent your resentment and disappointment.

- Some issues are greater than both of you. Attempting to constrain an answer can result in considerably more problems. Each individual works through issues in his or her own specific way. Keep in mind that you are partners, in good and in bad.

- Be open to change. Change is inevitable in life, and it will happen whether you run with it or battle it. Adaptability is crucial to adjust to change that is continually occurring in any relationship, and it permits you to develop together through both the great times and the terrible.

- Don't overlook issues. Whatever issues emerge in a relationship, it is paramount to face them together as a couple. In the event that a part of the relationship quits meeting expectations, don't essentially disregard it. Instead, address it with your partner. Things change, so react to them together as they do.

Many couples concentrate on their relationship just when there are particular, unavoidable issues to deal with. Once the issues have been determined, they regularly switch their concentration again to their professions, children, or daily errands. But relationships require constant nurturing and affection to thrive. As long as the soundness of a relationship is essential to you, it is going to require your consideration and care.

CHAPTER 11

Giving is Being

I do not recall a time in my life when I wasn't crazy busy. I've been trying to accomplish the next thing while barely living. It is really interesting to me. As a matter of fact, I just realized something.

Since I set my first goal in my life, I have been in this chain reaction of things while trying to survive for the next one. For the first five years, I did pretty well. High energy, totally pumped with adrenaline. Enjoying the extreme high that being intellectually sharp produces in you. Reaching ten years, it had already started to take a toll on me. By the time I hit twenty years, I was so depleted and exhausted! It was obvious something needed to change in my life just for me to stay alive.

But what?

I kept thinking and thinking. I didn't do much more than come up with some new goals and new things to do. Hoping that when accomplished, my life would skyrocket.

And this is the promise I would make to myself every time. That the outcome of the goals I set for myself would somehow change the way I feel about things. But guess what, it instead controlled the way I felt about myself.

I overworked my own needs to the point of exhaustion. Trying to accomplish so I could finally be. I put my health on the line many times to help others succeed. I handled a business that wasn't mine. I worked on new projects and ideas for others. Implemented, re-implemented. Tried this, tried that. All with the purpose of getting the love and attention I really craved. All I got back were offenses and more demands. Never got the love I was dying to receive.

For years I would not get what I needed. Yet I kept listening to the demands of others and kept working toward my impossible goal. I did not realize back then that I needed to be first before I could even enjoy the smallest of the successes.

I had forgotten how to be myself.

By not being, I certainly could not love deeply and profoundly. I could not communicate my soul's desires and intentions. I had lost myself. I had allowed myself to drift away from my core purpose. I stopped being the person who people really loved, authentically.

Fast forward to the day in my life in which I became myself again. It was such a relief to be welcomed back! To be loved by me and feel the real love from others for the first time ever.

As soon as I returned to myself, this book's inspiration came to me, all at once, as I walked to my hotel room after the last session of Date With Destiny. Everyone was coming to me to give me a hug. Pouring so much love into my heart that I simply sat down and wrote a book in twenty-something days.

Can you imagine how long it would have taken me to write a book if I had decided I wanted to become an author and started fishing for book ideas? It could have been as fast, sure. But certainly, I would have had to push myself a lot to make it.

I soared through this journey because I became it before I executed it. I crossed through the life lessons needed for the outcome to fall into my lap. And that's where you see the magic of the universe unfold in front of your eyes.

So I sat and watched. And looked up to heaven and thanked my own soul for this incredible opportunity to be aware of the light we've been given.

Words of Wisdom

Think about a goal in your life right now. What would happen when you achieve it? Why is achieving so important to you? It is amazing to work for goals, but do you celebrate your life, your success?

What would you do when the race is over? When you notice the exhausted, unfulfilled version of you is still waiting for you to show up? Are you pushing to get things done or are you soaring through your destiny while you work hard?

You need a quick shift of focus. A shift that generates unlimited energy for you and your projects. You won't need to push so hard to achieve things.

It might even feel that you have to carry yourself around from place to place. As if the emotional you had to convince itself over and over of the reasons you are doing something. I know it feels that way sometimes. And you push through it telling yourself it will be different this time.

You tell yourself that this time something new will happen. Someone will finally understand and notice your hard work, and then you will relax. Then you will take care of yourself, finally! But that never happens, does it? And you are at the end of your rope.

You might be even turning on yourself and starting to behave like the person you never wanted to be. You feel you need to stop but can't seem to figure out where to go from here.

Imagine you could tell yourself to walk and you would just go! Imagine if you could align that mind with that body, and your body would simply respond to your inner plan.

What is that part of us that resists and doesn't follow? Somehow, along the way, you tried to get rid of your internal enemy. Someone rejected you for a human trait you exposed and you classified it as not good. You marked it for deletion.

This is an unconscious process we all have running inside. We have been on the lookout for this internal enemy and been on a mission to destroy it.

This is the side we attempt to hide from others. We hide one side of us, the one we hate the most. Don't get rid of the enemy within, because even that is suicide.

Acknowledge it, love it. For meeting its needs is what you are missing to finally accept yourself. You will then stop looking for what you have been desperately seeking from the outside world. You will instead turn inward to meet your deepest needs.

When you are at your center,

the conflict ends.

Now what you do flows. It doesn't matter how difficult it could be, or how big the goals might be. You are now flying at the top of your wings. Now the goals pull you. You are truly attracted to your own life, your family, and others.

You are going to feel like gravity has become lighter, for you will be floating in the ecstasy of realization and deep understanding.

Stop doing to be.

Be, so you can really do.

The shift in focus is, in essence, the realization you will double, triple what you can do and achieve if you show up fully all the time. When you do not have to spend daily energy getting yourself to buy into your life again and again. Who wants that anyway?

Imagine you have to jumpstart your car every single day. For the first month, it's not a big deal, then you start hating it while telling yourself how grateful you should be you have a car in the first place. This is the internal conflict which stagnates us.

This feeling of having to drag yourself and, at the same time, feeling guilty for wanting more, can be applied to many areas of our lives. Even if you are extremely wealthy. If you achieved that success pushing yourself, you must have struggled through life. You might be proud of it, and that's how you allowed yourself to love you, and others might love you for it as well.

But are you fulfilled?

Trust me when I say you could have experienced more love and more satisfaction than what you have experienced up to this point. And it basically comes from the freedom of not expecting love, acceptance and appreciation as a reward for your achievements.

It's not that you won't have it, but rather that you give yourself the love, acceptance and appreciation before you go on the quest for success.

Giving is being.

From now on, you walk into goals with the love, the acceptance and the appreciation you thought you would receive when the goal was completed.

This is why visualization works. People imagine the result, and they tell you: feel like you would feel when the goal is achieved. The key word is to feel. It's not like some magic is going to happen and things will be suddenly done for you. It is that you are going to celebrate right now. You are happy now. You solve the conflicts that take energy away from the project before you start the project. You become whole and fulfilled just by having the chance to pursue the dream.

So now you know.

If you want to do X, become X, and the universe will conspire to make it happen.

Become your most precious desire. Then sit and watch how you will flow through your goals, and the hard work would be the marvelous journey you envisioned it would be.

Go become, and let's get doing.

CHAPTER 12

Changing How You Handle Conflict

"This really isn't the end of the world, Michelle." Tim's voice had the strained, high-pitched tone of caring turned to exasperation. "The microwave is fully functional, and we can't afford to go out to dinner every night while the kitchen gets repaired. It's just a burst pipe; you make it sound like the house is falling down around us. We can eat off paper plates while the kitchen sink's getting fixed, and for the thousandth time there's no significant risk of bacteria forming where the kitchen flooded." It had been two days since the pipe under the kitchen sink had burst, and it would be five days until the kitchen would be back in working order again. But Tim and Michelle were beginning to fear that it would take longer to repair the rupture that seemed to be widening between them.

"I don't understand how you can be so insensitive!" Michelle was near tears. "You know that I have OCD. You even read that book on it that my therapist recommended. You must know by now that if something is worrying me, I can't just put it out of my mind like you can. I can't stop thinking about how contaminated everything is. The workmen are leaving empty soda cans and fast-food wrappers in the kitchen where they're working, which, of course, attracts ants and cockroaches—maybe even rats. Am I the only one who cares about the children getting sick?" Michelle started to cry. "I'm already up to my eyeballs in stress, and now you're laying into me, too. I need you to be on my side, but you're on the firing squad instead."

"I'm not about to sit here and pretend that what you're saying is reasonable, Michelle," Tim volleyed back, as he walked out of the room. "If you're waiting for me to agree with you, you're going to be waiting a long time, because I just don't."

"Look, I have to take a time-out right now. I'm going to the bedroom." Michelle disappeared down the hall.

If you suffer from high anxiety, there's a good chance that you and your partner will react quite differently to various bumps in the road, just as Michelle and Tim had different reactions to the burst pipe in their kitchen. These differing reactions can give rise to ruptures in your sense of connection and partnership. When Tim was unable to corroborate Michelle's fears and perceptions, she responded by going on the attack, essentially giving him the message that he was an insensitive, inadequate partner. Tim shot back that Michelle, not he, was the one being unreasonable—getting in one last volley before walking out of the room and initiating the retreat. At this point, Michelle recognized that she was getting triggered, so she took a time-out, halting the destructive escalation of conflict between her and her partner.

Although it was said in a flurry of anger, Tim's final comment hit on a crucial truth, something that no amount of stress reduction on Michelle's part could change: he did not share her perspective. When you have anxiety and your partner does not, your viewpoints will often diverge. This divergence can give rise to conflicts that may worsen your anxiety or trigger other intense emotions, such as anger and hurt, as it did for Michelle. Yet how do you interact with your partner when conflict arises, without falling into familiar yet destructive communication patterns such as the attack and the retreat? Your divergent viewpoints will remain a source of rupture unless you allow room for both viewpoints to coexist. In this chapter you will gain the ability to honor your own feelings, fears, and perspectives, while simultaneously acknowledging and honoring those of your partner. This ability will make all the difference in shifting from reacting to intentionally responding to your partner, thereby helping you remain in connection with one another as you explore your differences.

Reactions vs. Intentional Responses

What is the difference between reacting and intentionally responding? As we see it, reactions are rash, intense responses to your partner. If you're in a reactive mode and you come into conflict with your partner, emotion—intense emotion, at that—will dictate your actions and words. It's not just anxiety that can get in your way. Anger, frustration, disappointment, and sadness, to name just a few emotions, can become just as overwhelming and destructive as your unchecked anxiety has been. This is because these emotions, even in the absence of anxiety, can lead to emotional flooding.

This emotional flooding will send your midbrain into hyperdrive. Just as when you become flooded with anxiety, the communication between your midbrain and your logic-based forebrain is impeded. Your emotions blast with the intensity of a megaphone, while your more-rational appraisals of your partner and your situation barely have the attention getting power of a whisper. Emotions escalate, conflict intensifies, and you find yourself embroiled in either the attack or the retreat with your partner, simply because reactions, whether they are fueled by fear or another emotion, have run amok. A sense of connection and partnership is again lost.

Intentional responses, on the other hand, are not governed by a tidal wave of unrestrained emotion. When you're intentionally responding to your partner, both the emotional and cognitive systems of your brain are online and communicating fluently with one another. When both you and your partner are able to access this emotionally grounded and neurologically balanced state during a conflict, interpersonal communication can flow freely. This is because you're able to let both emotion and rational thought inform your actions and your responses to your partner. As a result, you and your partner can experience a sense of connection and attunement—even in the face of conflict. No longer embroiled in the uncontained reactions of attack and retreat, you have the mental and emotional flexibility to value both your and your partner's differing perspectives.

Moving from Reacting to Intentionally Responding

The first step in moving from reacting to intentionally responding is to interrupt your reactions. When you notice yourself slipping into a reactive mode, you can use a time-out to interrupt the reaction and de-escalate your emotional flooding. After the time-out, when you've regained your sense of calm, you can respond first to your needs and then to the needs of your partner. With the tools provided in this chapter, you will learn to identify your unmet needs during conflict with your partner. Next, you will acknowledge the vulnerable feelings that the conflict elicited and begin to nurture yourself and ease your distress. Finally, you then will apply the communication skills of mirroring and validation, taught later, to engage your partner powerfully and effectively. In so doing, you will transform your experience of conflict. If your partner is learning the mirroring and validation tools as well, you will have more of a common ground to start from. However, even if your partner is not familiar with these tools, your relationship will still benefit greatly by your employing them.

Putting Conflict on Hold with a Time-Out

Anxiety can not only bring about fear, panic, and nervousness, but also lead to conflict in your relationship, as was the case with Tim and Michelle. At this point in the game, you're already skilled at identifying the cognitive, emotional, and physical indicators of your anxiety. You're also well practiced at taking a time-out when these red flags arise and returning to a state of equilibrium with your time-out techniques. Now you can begin applying the time-outs to de-escalate your emotional reactivity during interactions with your partner.

<u>Exercise 5</u> Take a Time-Out When You Are Emotionally Triggered

When you notice the following red-flag emotions intensifying during interactions with your partner, it's time for a time-out.

Anger

Despair

Exhaustion

Failure

Fear

Frustration

Impatience

Inadequacy

Irritability

Isolation

Loneliness

Nervousness

Overwhelm

Panic

Resentment

Sadness

Shame

Once you've completed your time-out exercises, communication between your forebrain and midbrain will be reestablished. You'll be able to calmly evaluate the emotions that set you off, then take the next step: giving yourself the emotional reassurance you need. The next exercise teaches you how to do just that.

Identifying Your Unmet Needs and Meeting Them

Regardless of the specifics of your conflict with your partner—what he said or didn't say, did or didn't do—your hurt or anger, when you get to its root, stems from your desire for connection with your partner. And that desire wasn't met. Missing were the qualities of connection: gentleness, attentiveness, care, a sense of partnership, and the reassuring feeling that you're not alone in your distress.

Those with whom we're most intimately connected have the power to hurt us the most. The emotional connection we experience with our partners is so powerful that its absence is profoundly painful. More often than not, we don't recognize that it's this loss of connection that causes us to react with criticism, defensiveness, contempt, or stonewalling—behaviors that relationship expert John Gottman (1994) calls the "Four Horsemen of the Apocalypse" of a partnership. Now that you know that a loss of connection lies behind your intense reactions to your partner's words or behavior, you can identify the specific trigger that ruptured the connection.

Although the loss of connection is painfully palpable, you will discover, through the following exercise, that you can be okay even though the needs that you want your partner to fulfill aren't met all the time. This is empowering. In reality, no one is able to meet all of your needs all of the time. The good news from this realization is that you aren't completely dependent on others for your soothing and validation. You can give yourself the gift of self-compassion, self-soothing, and self-understanding. While receiving care from your partner is an essential component of any good relationship, self-care is essential as well. You can provide yourself with some of the comfort, care, and emotional support that you yearn for.

Exercise 5.2 Identify and Meet Your Emotional Needs

In this exercise you will first identify your emotional needs and then learn how you yourself can meet those needs, when necessary, with acceptance, compassion, and self-validation.

After you have calmed yourself with your stress-reducing techniques, and before you end your time-out, take the following steps:

1.   Remember what your partner did or said during your last interaction that triggered your reaction.

2.   Shift your focus from the conflict itself to the feelings it stirred in you. You can refer back to the list of emotional triggers in the previous exercise to help you identify the emotions that arose for you.

3.   Now that you've identified your feelings, reflect on and identify the underlying need or longing that your partner didn't meet. You can use the following list to spur your thinking.

comfort

companionship

feeling attractive

feeling desired

feeling heard

feeling important

feeling needed

feeling respected

feeling unburdened

feeling understood

feeling valued

feeling worthy

partnership

safety

support

- Now that you've identified your unmet needs during that interaction, take a moment to give yourself the particular support that you were yearning for. To do so, get in touch with that wise-parent part of yourself that you learned to access in exercise 3.3. To get in touch with this wise-parent self, think back to times when you've shown that care and concern for others. The wise parent is that strong, nurturing part of yourself that is receptive, caring, and supportive—not judging, shaming, or criticizing. Now imagine showing that same care and concern for yourself that you've shown for others.

- Think of a statement that you would have liked to hear from your partner: the caring, loving response to your distress that you wanted but didn't get. If you like, get a pen and some paper, and write the words down.

- Imagine the vulnerable part of you standing in front of you. With the loving, affirming voice of your wise-parent self, silently repeat the statement that you yearned to hear.

- Cross your arms and embrace yourself, allowing the wise parent to comfort the part of you that feels vulnerable and in need. Give yourself this comfort for as long as you wish.

- When you've given yourself sufficient comfort and validation, take a deep breath, put your thumb and forefinger together making an "okay" symbol with your hand, and say to yourself, I'm okay. By doing this you are creating a cue that will automatically re-elicit the comfort and support of your wise-parent self. And know that at any time during your interactions with your partner, you can put your thumb and forefinger together and use this cue to remind yourself that you're okay. And because you are okay, you can be in control of your reactions. In this way you can always provide yourself the care, comfort, and self-support that you need.

- Bring your time-out to a close, knowing that just because your time-out is ending, your self-care doesn't need to stop. With the knowledge that you have a multitude of self-care tools at your fingertips, you can now return from your time-out and check in with your partner.

Initiating Dialogue with Your Partner

Now that you are calm and have given yourself validation, you're in an optimal state of mind to communicate with your partner. Your baseline stress level is back in the green zone, you're emotionally on firmer ground, and you can be intentionally responsive rather than reactive in conversation. Because you have already provided yourself with some of the comfort and understanding that you wanted from your partner, you're less likely to become emotionally flooded again when discussing this need with your partner, as you'll learn how to do next.

By approaching your partner now, you have the opportunity to repair any ruptures that occurred before your time-out. The first step in the repair process is asking your partner if it's a good time to talk. Unlike you, your partner hasn't necessarily just had a time-out for self-soothing, so you want to ensure that your partner is in an open, responsive frame of mind when you resume your dialogue.

If your partner doesn't feel that it's a good time to talk, decide on a time during the next twenty-four hours, if possible, when you will sit down together to continue your interaction. When you do resume the conversation, make sure that you both are in a calm state. It's important that neither of you is too stressed, tired, or distracted to give the other your attention.

Exercise 5.3 Constructively Communicate Your Needs

When you and your partner do feel that it's a good time to talk, initiate dialogue following these three steps:

1. Start with the positive, stating what you appreciate about your partner.

2. Share the feeling you identified as painful, your partner's action that led to the feelings, and the deeper feeling of vulnerability in you that it elicited. Use the following strategies for constructive communication:

a. Use "I" statements. Express your feelings and experiences using the pronoun "I." For example, "I felt frustrated when you told me there's nothing to worry about. When you said that, I felt so alone," "I felt disconnected when you refused to spend any more time discussing my concern and you just turned back to your computer. I felt so unimportant to you," or "I felt shame when you said I was overreacting. When you said that, I wanted to just disappear."

b. Focus on your own feelings; don't make assumptions regarding your partner's thoughts or intentions, as in, "I know you think I'm overreacting," or "I know you think I'm a hypochondriac." Instead, stick to what you were feeling, as in, "I want you to understand how scared I get when…"

c. Keep it short and sweet. This dialogue works better if you are succinct in your communication. Your partner is more likely to receive your message if you use only a couple of sentences. Too much information makes it hard for your partner to take in and remember what you said.

3. Ask for your partner's feedback and response to what you've just shared by saying something like, "I'm open to your feedback and response to what I've just shared with you." After listening to your partner's response, use the mirroring and validation tools taught next. Throughout this conversation with your partner, remember that you are using new dialogue skills that your partner may lack. Nevertheless, you may be pleased to discover how much the tone of your interaction changes when you bring effective communication skills to the table.

Developing Active Listening Skills: Mirroring

Couples therapy experts and authors Harville Hendrix and Helen Hunt (1994) have said that the first requirement of love is listening. Unfortunately, most of us have not developed very good listening skills. We get too caught up in our own thoughts, feelings, and responses to hear accurately what our partners are saying to us. We often place too much focus on ourselves and, in doing so, fail to really hear the other. When this occurs, we fall prey to what we call the "three I's of miscommunication": inattention, interrupting, and interjecting.

INATTENTION

When you are listening to another person, it's natural to be distracted by the running commentary in your own head. While your partner is talking, you probably find yourself thinking about what you want to say next or reflecting on your opinion of what your partner is saying. You are busy evaluating and judging your partner's point of view. This is not conducive to building a sense of connection and to promoting mutual understanding in your relationship. When you listen to your own internal running commentary, you don't actually hear what your partner is saying. Or you might hear some of it but miss some crucial points. This inattention, more often than not, leads to misinterpretation. Making matters worse, you may often react to those misinterpretations, becoming emotionally triggered by what you think your partner is telling you without checking to make sure that your interpretation is correct.

INTERRUPTING AND INTERJECTING

Interruption and interjection go hand in hand. Whether you wait until your partner stops talking or cut in midsentence, you are interrupting by immediately interjecting your own thoughts, feelings, and opinions. When you interrupt your partner, you're not giving her the time and space to be fully heard. This is counter to the goal of openness and receptivity. Whether you're jumping to conclusions, misinterpreting your partner's words, changing the subject, or trying to piggyback on what you believe your partner is expressing, you're not considering and valuing your partner's opinion. The connection you seek to establish through the dialogue can be destroyed in this way.

While your partner is speaking, there may be times when you feel anxious that you won't have a chance to express your opinion. This is a common feeling, especially when you first begin practicing the mirroring technique. When these fears arise, know that you, too, will have a turn to speak. Expressing your own response to your partner is just as important as actively listening to her viewpoint, but if you skip over the listening stage, immediately thinking about and expressing your own response, you're denying your partner the very experience of being heard that you yourself crave.

Exercise 5.4 Mirroring

Two crucial components of the process of communication are giving your partner a chance to communicate what he needs to say and checking to make sure that you have understood what your partner said. This is what's done in mirroring. You listen attentively to your partner and then "reflect" this communication by restating what you believe your partner has said to you. Finally, you check to see if you "got it right," giving your partner a chance to clarify anything you might have missed and confirming what you correctly understood. If you bypass these three fundamental steps, you increase the likelihood of miscommunication, heightened emotional activation, and renewed conflict. Learning and applying the following three steps of mirroring is a simple, concrete way to avoid falling prey to the three "I's" of miscommunication.

Step 1: Listen to your partner. While your partner is speaking, don't divert your attention by thinking about:

- How you're going to respond
- How what your partner is saying is wrong
- How your opinion is right

Instead, cultivate an attitude of curiosity:

- Welcome what your partner shares with you.
- Appreciate the novelty and uniqueness of your partner's perspective, just as you would appreciate the novelty of exploring a foreign culture.

- If you notice that your stress is on the rise, take a few deep breaths or initiate some four-square breathing as you continue to listen. Doing some calming breath work can help you maintain the attitude of openness and curiosity you are working to cultivate.

Actively placing all of your attention on simply taking in what your partner is saying can be frustrating if you think your partner has the facts all wrong. Just remember, correcting facts is not the goal. The goal is to offer careful attention and precise listening to your partner as she attempts to communicate with you.

Step 2: Reflect. When your partner finishes speaking, begin your response by saying, "Let me see if I understood everything you just said. You said that…" Then repeat back what your partner just communicated to you as close to verbatim as you can. You probably won't get it perfect, but try to get the gist of what you heard your partner say. In reflecting your partner's words calmly and caringly, you convey that you are making an earnest effort to listen.

Step 3: Do a content check. When you've repeated what you think your partner said, ask, "Did I get that right?"

Good communication is not about proving who is right, but about making the effort to really hear one another. Mirroring shows your partner that you are making that effort, that you listened closely to what she said and want to understand it—even if you disagree. Once you have done this, you're ready for the next step of constructive communication: validating your partner's point of view and experience.

Validating Your Partner

It's only human to wish that your partner always agreed with you, saw the world just as you see it, and shared your opinions, feelings, and convictions. But this just doesn't happen. While the uniqueness of every person can lend variety and excitement to relationships, it can also be a source of contention, frustration, and disconnect. You and your partner will sometimes disagree or have trouble even understanding your differences. By validating your partner following his communication, you acknowledge that his thoughts and feelings make sense, given his perspective. This doesn't mean that you necessarily agree with your partner's perspective, but that you can look at it from your partner's viewpoint and validate it. You give equal value to the different points of view that you and your partner hold.

According to psychologist Alan Fruzzetti (2006), validation conveys understanding and acceptance of your partner. By validating your partner's point of view, you are acknowledging and honoring your different viewpoints. The key to mastering validation is to embrace the reality that you can validate another person's thoughts and feelings even if your opinions are in direct opposition to them. This is why validating your partner can be challenging. Recognizing that your partner has very different opinions, reactions, emotions, and interests than you do can cause anxiety. You may be afraid that it means you're wrong (when you know you aren't) or that the two of you won't be able to stay together. On the contrary, for your relationship to work, you both need to accept that you are unique, separate individuals and give each other the space to express your individuality. Validation offers you a way to honor this essential separateness by acknowledging that two opposing viewpoints can coexist: one needn't invalidate the other.

It can also be especially difficult to practice validation because, since you suffer from anxiety, you're probably emotionally exhausted. You may just want reassurance from your partner and feel unable to offer validation to him. The act of listening to and validating your partner, however, can lessen your anxiety by shifting your focus outside of yourself. This is an important step in mastering your anxiety. Happily, at the same time it does wonders for your relationship.

CHAPTER 13

Relationship Mistakes You Don't Want to Repeat

We've determined if you're truly ready to get back out into the dating world or if you want to turn your disastrous dating around. We've worked through building up your self-confidence for a better dating experience. This chapter talks about knowing what kind of a man you're looking for and what kind of a relationship you want to have.

In this chapter, we will cover the many mistakes and the missteps we all have made in our dating lives and need to avoid repeating if we must succeed in this game.

How often have you started dating a man thinking it was going to go somewhere only to find out that he has no plans to go to the next level? Many women waste years on the wrong guy. They assume the relationship will become permanent and are afraid to ask the hard questions. The truth is, he never had any intention of committing to you. By then you may have invested years of your life into this man.

Here is another scenario. He tells you he's not interested in a committed relationship, but you're convinced you can change his mind. You're thinking of all the time you've spent together, and you don't want to give up now. The sad part is, one day he up and leaves you.

There are many devastating dating disasters like that. We are women forty, fifty, sixty years old and older who have never learned how to be good at dating and having quality relationships. Unfortunately, as a result, we've also had more divorces than ever.

As a dating coach I ask women about their conversations on dates, especially on the first date. Their stories tell me how little they manage to learn about that man. I've asked women who've been with a man for six months and longer the same question, and the result is the same: they never ask the kinds of questions that would allow them to get to know their man. I've had women say they didn't want to be accused of asking too many questions. Getting to know someone is not about asking too many questions, it's about being smart. If you're thinking about spending your life with someone, you need to find out everything you can about them. You need to determine as quickly as possible if he would be a good fit for you.

I'll tell you what's nosy. Nosy is asking to see his tax returns, his credit report, his bank statements; nosy is asking about the value of his house or whether or not he owns one. Nosy is asking him how many women he'd slept with, which is none of your business, nor should any man ever be asking you that question either.

The opposite extreme is not asking enough questions. I call it the interrogation. Conducting an interrogation is not the right approach. I've known women who show up on their first date with a laundry list of questions, their mission to extract as much information from their date as possible. That turns men off. Can you blame them?

So how do you go about finding the middle of the road and learning all you can about your guy the right way? The right way is to spend quality time with one another and have typical conversations that include good questions. How many of us have been afraid to speak up and ask for what we want? How many of us have allowed the men in our lives to call the shots? How many of us have done things we didn't want to do, but we did them because the man in our life wanted it and told us what to do? How many of us have slept with dates because we didn't know how to say no, or because he wanted sex and we were all about pleasing the man? How many of woman became pregnant because their man didn't want to take precautions and later left them to be a single parent? How many of us have contracted STDs because our partners or husbands were unfaithful? The answer to all of these questions is, most of us. We just went along with it all, never asking the right questions, never asking our dates for test results or asking whether or not they'd been checked by a doctor.

If you're about to share your most intimate self with a man, you have a right to know and to request this information.

How many women have been left because they no longer had the body they had when they got married? We've had his children, and he still wanted us to be a size 10. How many times have men disrespected us and left us feeling worthless and powerless? How many were told repeatedly by their spouses that we were nothing and that no one would want them. And worse yet, how many of us have tolerated physical abuse and suffered broken noses and black eyes? How many of us have stayed in alcohol- and drug-infused households because men needed us to take care of them? We've stayed because we were afraid to leave. Meanwhile, our children were traumatized daily by witnessing the horrors of addiction.

Most of these scenarios began early in our relationships. They were traps, and we became victims. We didn't know better, and we didn't know how to recognize the trouble ahead.

How many of us have asked a man for a date, picked up the tab, and bought gifts—all in the vain attempt to get some guy to like us? We've offered sex to someone because we believed that would get us the guy. How many of us have chased relentlessly after a man we just couldn't let go of? How many of us haven't valued, loved, or respected ourselves? How many of us see ourselves in the destructive scenarios above? You can only make a change if you acknowledge it first.

I'm here to change lives.

I'm here to teach you not to repeat the destructive behaviors you've committed when you were younger. I'm one with you. I've made mistakes like this as too, until one day I realized I mattered. The time had come to love and to respect myself in a way I never knew how to before. My life had changed, my world had changed, and I became happier than I'd ever been. I what the same for you.

I hurt for myself, for you, and for women all over the world, women who didn't know how to do better. I want you to know that you're beautiful and magnificent, and that you can have a wonderful man and a fulfilling relationship in your life. Relationships are what life is about.

As a life coach I've learned about the challenge's women face in the dating world. It's all about being smarter the second time around. The greatest transformations and changes take place when we address our core issues. It's a light bulb moment. We see how we keep repeating our old patterns and keep engaging in our old behaviors. We keep choosing the same kind of man over and over again. His name is different, and he may be taller or shorter, but the life in each relationship will be pretty much the same. If you've chosen right the first time, you wouldn't be reading this book. You're someone who wants help in the dating world. I want your unhealthy destructive cycle broken. That instant attraction, that chemistry—it's the cycle you need to break. I've learned that it's almost always trouble. The best kind of attraction and chemistry develops over time, while you're getting to know your man. Most of us find men very handsome or attractive after we've gotten to know them. It's not always their looks, it can be their personality and charm that make them desirable.

We've all known the gorgeous Adonis-type who has left us breathless on the first date, and then later found out that he has no personality and is a total bore. He has relied on his looks all his life and has never developed an engaging personality, has never learned how to be an interesting conversationalist. We often wondered what we saw in him, because he no longer seemed attractive to us.

I've known women who made quick judgments on a date if the attraction wasn't immediate. They ruled out the man, deciding they're not interested. I encourage you to have at least two if not three dates before you make such a decision. I could show you how to dress and to act on a date, how to find that available quality man; I could teach you how to get to know him and learn the important things about him. However, I want to dig much deeper. I want to get to the heart of your conditioning and bring it to surface, to make you aware of your past, of how it has shaped you, and how you can change it.

It starts with building self-esteem and with creating standards.

Once we change how we think and feel about ourselves, we automatically start setting different standards. Some may say I'm old-school about this, but there is nothing old-school about having standards and respecting yourself. What is old-school is women who are still on a self-destructive path. It's important to address your past conditioning and programming to prepare you for a shift in your mindset so that you can move forward. By the end of this book you'll feel like a different person, a person who will know how to find that amazing man, a man who'll treat you like you're the best thing that's ever happened to him, a man who'll value, respect, and love you like you never dreamed possible.

Next we're going to talk about your first date. You know, the one that scares you to death. You're nervous, you don't know what to wear, you change your outfit so many times, your entire closest in on your bed by the time you finally settle on something. You're hoping he's going to like you. I want you to start thinking, "Are you going to like him?"

CHAPTER 14

Self-Work

When it comes to self-work, no one person is the same. What inspires change in one person may not resonate with another. Some of us need therapists, others medication. Some need good friends or supportive parents/mentors/caretakers. Others of us prefer to go it alone, using books, the internet, or journaling. Some of us need religion or spiritual connection to help us, and others find support groups to be sources of healing. There are so many different ways to "work on yourself", but when you are in the throws of chaos, it can be hard to know where to start. In this chapter I want to talk about where to start working on yourself, as well as some specific areas to focus on that will help you with your attachment system issues.

Starting Points

Chances are you've already started working on yourself. Every time you self-reflect in a journal/blog entry, talk to a friend, read a book, or try to have a real conversation with your partner you are indirectly unofficially working on yourself. To me, the difference between these informal ways of growing and changing, and really working on yourself, is a matter of focus and intention. When I talk about working on yourself in this book, I'm talking about digging deep and sorting out those issues which keep you from being happy and feeling worthy of love.

Five Starting Points for Working on Yourself

If you're ready to start the process, but don't know where to begin, here are some suggestions.

Therapy - Yes, therapy again. Counsellors are trained to help you work on yourself! If you have no clue where to start, find a therapist and they can help you determine what you want to work on and help you do it. One of the most beneficial aspects of going to a therapist is that they can listen and reflect back to you patterns that you can't objectively see. This is why visiting a therapist is a great starting place. You may go in with what you think is the issue, but with their help, discover the real problem that you need to address.

Books, Blogs, YouTube - Self-help books are relatively cheap, easy to get, and can be approached in whatever way is most helpful to you. You can choose based on recommendations or subject matter. You can piece together relevant quotes and ideas for yourself. I've read books from which I only related to one or two paragraphs, but those small pieces made a huge difference in my thinking. Take advantage of both physical and digital libraries, and build up a collection of your own resources from which to help yourself.

Blogs and YouTube channels are another cheap form of self-help. There are some amazing YouTube channels run by licensed therapists, and many well researched blogs. As with any other form of self-help, be careful of who you choose to listen to. If their advice makes you feel ashamed, guilty, or stupid, move on. Good self-help advice should challenge you, maybe even make you uncomfortable, but should always inspire positive changes.

Support Groups - Louise, who lost her husband to suicide, joined a support group to deal with the grief. It was the best decision she ever made. It got her through the first year after, and inspired her to become an advocate for suicide prevention. Interacting with others who struggle with the same issues can be a catalyst for growth and change. There is nothing quite like sitting with people who are in different stages of the journey and learning from them. They can spark ideas for growth and change, keep you accountable, and provide feedback when needed. There are support groups for almost every issue people have, some in - person and others online. Find one and see if it helps you.

Write - If you like to journal, begin journaling. Talk about your feelings and problems openly, and themes will begin to emerge. These can be areas of work for you. Another approach is to begin writing your story in narrative form. Write about experiences that shaped you. This will identify areas you might want to explore within yourself. You'll be surprised at the things that stick out as important that you thought didn't affected you much. Writing your life as a story also helps examine those experiences, in different ways, which helps you see patterns more clearly.

Ask a Trusted Source - This must be a person who you trust, and who you know will not lie to you. Someone who is secure and has your best interests at heart. Ask them to honestly tell you what behaviors they've seen you engage in that have caused problems in your life. You may have to find the right wording. You want to ask questions that you are ready to hear the answers to, and that will help you face the truth of situations that you haven't wanted to face. Picking the right person to ask can be tricky. They need to be secure enough to tell you the truth, even if it hurts, but not cruel. However, if you are able to find the right person and, they can help open your eyes to some patterns or behaviors you hadn't noticed before.

Areas of Focus for Self-Work

Below are five areas of focus that are common to those of us with anxious attachment systems. I introduce them here in the hopes that you can branch out and explore them further . You can easily find resources on these topics. Let's take a look at the topics that will be most helpful to explore on your self-work journey.

Family of Origin

No surprise here folks. You will have to look at your family of origin when doing work on yourself. Many people think they can skip this topic, or they minimize events that happened to them when they were young, because they don't believe it could still affect them. The truth is that our childhoods shaped us and as we can see from attachment theory, we develop most of our attachment patterns in early childhood. We also inherit, genetically and behaviourally, patterns from our family. To understand ourselves, we have to look at those who shaped us, and those who shaped them. Once you begin to look at your family of origin, you will more fully understand some of your behaviors and where they come from. This is probably the most difficult and entrenched area of self-work, but an important one nonetheless. It's not about blaming your parents or opening old wounds. You're goal with family of origin work is to understand how you came to be the way you are, and figure out how to go about changing what you want to change.

Inner child work

Now, this may be too woo woo for some of you, but it's area to explore. Those us with insecure attachment systems lacked secure and consistent nurturing as children. One approach to helping us fill this void as adults is be to our "inner child" what our caretakers couldn't be for us then. Some people do this on a surface level. They may step in when negative self-talk begins. As an example. You say to yourself I'm such an idiot! Why did I call him? I am so stupid and worthless. If you are doing inner child work, you might stop yourself and interrupt as a loving parent and say, I know you're upset, but you are not stupid. You are very smart, you just got overwhelmed and made a bad choice. It is a way of hearing what we wished we had heard growing up. For more deep seated issues, I've read that people keep pictures of themselves as children, and talk to themselves to work through the trauma with the support they never received . This is just a glimpse into inner child work. It may feel weird at first, but I do recommend looking into this area to see if it can help you work on some of your issues.

Co-dependency/ Addiction Issues

Many of us with anxious attachment systems also have co-dependency or addiction issues. There are volumes written about these two subjects, so I won't spend too much time here. However, I do want to say that sometimes addiction sneaks in in ways that we wouldn't expect. Maybe you don't have a drinking or drug problem, but I'll bet as an anxious you've developed some other kind of addiction that has helped you cope with the feelings you've faced during your life. I recommend reading about addiction in general, and doing some self-reflection to determine if you have any areas in your life that you've used to cover for feelings of inadequacy or being unlovable. Be honest and if you discover any specific types of addiction for yourself, look further into them.

Self-Esteem

Many people suffer from lack of self-esteem, but anxiously attached people even more so. I think our issues go a little deeper than just lacking confidence, but nonetheless, it may be helpful for you to look into this topic. So, me books out there give you skills and cognitive tools that can help you build that outer confidence, to help you fake it till you make it. We can all use tools that help us feel better about ourselves. If you can identify areas that you excel in, then you will have an area of focus when you are feeling low. For me, that is writing and baking. For you, it could be your ability to build miniatures, fix cars, brew homemade beer, or garden. Finding things about yourself that you appreciate or excel at that give you something to fall back on when a relationship doesn't work out.

Trauma

The last area of focus is trauma. Trauma is a broad category. It can refer to big traumas, like mental, physical, or sexual abuse, neglect, or death. Trauma can refer to divorce, natural disasters, or war. Trauma can also refer to events that may not seem big to others, but which impacted us enough to change how we related to the world. To truly heal yourself you have to back through your life and figure out what these traumatic events were for you, and figure out how to work through them. Forgetting, denying, minimizing, and ignoring only serves to drive the traumatic event into the subconscious, leading to acting out behaviors that, because we don't acknowledge the trauma, seem inexplicable . It can also cause us to stay in a victim role, where we cannot open up and experience the joys in life because we are stuck in the pain. In self - work, you find a way to acknowledge the trauma and integrate the experience, so that you give it the gravity it deserves, but you are able to function in a healthy way as well. There are plenty of resources on trauma, but I recommend a therapist's help for this one, especially if you've experienced one of the "big T" traumas. No matter what, trauma is going to come up in self-work, and it's' very important to follow your process for working through it.

The Good News, and the Bad

This process of self-work can take years, and it doesn't have an endpoint. It isn't a mapped-out course that has defined measurable objectives, and there is no date of completion where you will graduate with a degree in happiness. I tell you this because when you start working on yourself things will get complicated. You will go through periods of numbness and exhaustion, or tears and frustration. If you are really doing the work, you will find there are times of feeling elated and enlightened, followed by doubt and backtracking. You may focus intensely for months, then take a break for a year. Relationships will change. You will feel like you don't know yourself. You will experience a lot of pain in letting go of old coping mechanisms that have kept you "safe". But, as you begin to replace those old habits with healthy new ones, you will find that you are indeed happier. You will feel more capable and less like a victim. You will know that you are making your own decisions and come to terms with your past, present, and future.

Life may still not turn out as you expected. Your prince charming may never come. You will still have issues with co-workers, parents, and siblings. You will still have days where your old habits pop back up, but you will find that you can stop them more quickly and easily. What used to be three months of depression and obsession after a breakup, will turn into a week. What used to be extreme anger and resentment at a partner being late, will turn into disappointment, followed by an acceptance and a decision to continue interacting with that person or not. You will be less afraid of conflict, and speak your mind without fearing how others will react. Everything will seem a little clearer and you will not second guess your thoughts and feelings. You will validate yourself. I believe this is the "secret" of happy and secure people. They aren't perfect, they aren't better or more loveable than you, they just grew up knowing how to believe in themselves. You had to learn it the hard way.

CONCLUSION

Pulling It All Together

Before you go back into the scary world of dating, I have a few more tips to give you, to leave you fully armed and ready for your dating success.

First and foremost, dating success starts with you and how you feel about yourself. Until you feel comfortable in your own skin, you'll struggle.

In the beginning of the book we've talked about enhancing your appearance. Sometimes that's all it takes. If you look fabulous when you look in the mirror, it can create a 180-degree shift in how you feel on the inside. If you want a man to treat you like a queen, you must like yourself and treat yourself that way first.

I've given you the tools to help you take the first steps back into the dating world. I want to carry that a bit further before I wrap up the book by giving you a few more strategies to ensure your dating success.

Our demographic has passed through decades of building bad habits. We don't seem to have learned much from that, and too many of us are still making mistakes. We must change how we do things to give us a different and better results.

Do you remember the times when girls were asking men for dates? Men loved it. They didn't have to do much and certainly didn't have to face being rejected as they did when they had to do the asking. As a result, men became very lazy and stopped trying to pursue the girls of their choice. So many girls have asked them for dates, most of these men at some point got lucky and married one of the girls who had been pursuing them. Many of these men are now single and out in the dating world again, clueless as to how to do the pursuing. They're still waiting for the women to make their first move. And you know what? Some women are still doing it.

Don't you want the man to do the work for you? The more a man works to win a woman's heart, the more he values her. Aren't we all about finding a quality man who cherishes and adores us? Then we have to play our cards differently. I'm not suggesting playing games here—we're too old for games. What I'm saying is, if we were to get what we want and to have what we want, we have to engage in more effective ways.

If a man were to have me because I've pursued him, I would probably never feel valued or special in some way. But I would feel it if he really worked at winning me and at selling himself to me. I'd think, "Yes, I'm special, and he has played his cards well. He has showed me that he has what it takes to make me happy, to provide for me and to take care of me." That's what you want. When you start dating again, let the men pursue you. There is nothing wrong with flirting and showing an interest, but they must make the first move.

Another bad habit that came out of the same era is us women picking up the tab. We would pay for half the dinner bill, or too many times we would pick up the entire bill. One of the hardest jobs as a coach I have is to get women to keep their credit cards in their handbags. If the man does the inviting, then the man pays. There is only one time when you can be the one paying, and that's to reciprocate and to occasionally treat him. Most men—if they're true gentlemen—still won't allow you pay, but they'll certainly appreciate your efforts to do something for them. However, if you have a man or several men whom you've known for some time and you're just friends, I'd say it's okay to share in the expense of your entertainment. But I don't recommend it if you're looking for the quality man you want a relationship with.

Here is my philosophy. I want a man who is generous and who shows me he wants to take care of me, and that includes paying. I'm not interested in being invited to a dinner and being expected to pay for part of the evening on a date this man has asked me for. If a man asks you to pay for half, he's not the quality man you're looking for. No, no, no. You're not to make an excuse that he doesn't have much money. If he can't afford the cost of a date, he shouldn't be asking you for company, period.

Dating in the second half of your life is all about making good choices. Do you really want to take on supporting yourself and another person too? Some of the women I've coached have dated men outside of the area where they live. A few of these women had made their own travel arrangements and had paid for the trips to see their men. Their men had it easy and rarely made the trips themselves. Often, I've been around to see these one-sided relationships end.

The first time a man expects you to travel to meet him, you have to let him know what you expect from him. It will be tough to do, but you must do it. Here is what you say: "I'd love to come and see you. Can I expect you to make the travel arrangements and pay for the trip? It's the only way I'd be able to come and see you. Or maybe it's easier for you to make the trip and visit me? I'd love to see you." Believe me, you'll find out very quickly what you need to know about this man. A real gentleman would never even cause you to have to say that. A real gentleman will invite you and will let you know that he's making all your travel arrangements and that the tab is on him. He's a man who shows respect and values you. The same holds true for the man who is suggesting a weekend getaway. A real gentleman will say, "I'll have two rooms reserved for us." He will let you know upfront that he's not expecting anything you're not ready for. If he wants to take you away for the weekend and says nothing about the accommodations, you must ask him and let him know that you must have your own room. If he expects you to pay for the extra room, don't accept his invitation.

I'm reminding you again—you're looking for a quality man who will respect you, value you, and take care of you.

Our demographic has had our share of boyfriends in our earlier years, and some of us have done a reasonable amount of bed-hopping. That's another bad habit we have developed.

Unfortunately, it's a pattern the young women of today have taken on as a norm. Physical intimacy is happening too quickly. For years I've been encouraging my clients to slow down. There are a number of reasons for this.

Comedian and The Steve Harvey Morning Show host Steve Harvey came up with the ninety-day rule.3 The ninety-day rule is a decision you make when dating a man not to have sex for at least ninety days. I think it's an excellent advice as it takes you at least that amount of time to get to know the man you're dating. If you start having sex a week or two into dating, it will cloud your thinking, and you'll miss what you really should be concentrating on, and that's getting to know the man you're with. In ninety days you'll only manage to scratch the surface of his true personality, but once you bring sex into the relationship, your focus will stray.

I want to leave you with one of the best pieces of advice I've ever gotten—take your time with physical intimacy. If he's the one for you, develop the emotional intimacy first—it'll make everything so much better when you do become physically intimate. There is so much you need to find out about this man. Will he stay around if he's not having sex with you? Is he clean? Will he get himself tested before you have sex? There are more STDs in the senior population than has ever been reported.

Guard your health and be cautious. I've had women ask me how to say no. Here is how you do it. Simply say, "I'm not ready to go there yet, give me time." If the man pouts and doesn't respect that, he's not the man for you, and it's best to reevaluate. I've also known women who don't want anything permanent. They like the freedom of dating different men and experiencing variety. They enjoy having sex with whomever they choose.

I'm not old school, and I'm not a prude. We all have the freedom and the dignity to live our lives as we choose, and no one has the right to tell us otherwise.

I know what you're thinking. You're thinking, "But I want to know if we're compatible!" If you take your time and get to know each other, you'll know if you're a fit. Spend weekends together, take trips, travel. You don't have to go so far as to live together. Once you do, chances are great there will be no marriage. On the other hand, if you're a couple that is happy together, and if you both understand that marriage is not the goal, then it's okay. It's a convenient arrangement for couples in their eighties and nineties that want their assets and estates to go to their children.

You develop standards by knowing what you want and what's important to you. Once they're clear in your mind, you'll find it very easy to recognize the right man for you. If your bar is high, you'll find the man who will rise to the occasion and meet your standards. Anything less will leave you unsatisfied. This is why it's so important to set your standards first. Once you hold yourself to a standard, you'll know what's necessary for you and what you want in that special man. Don't let anyone tell you that you've set your bar too high. Remember, it's your life, and you can have what's important to you, because you're worth it.

I hold myself to very high standards, and I'd expect nothing less from the man in my life. A man loves the woman who has standards. It takes the guesswork out for him. He knows what's important to her and he'll meet her expectations. Please don't waste time on the men who are not what you're looking for. I know some women who became good friends with the men they came to like, the men who weren't fit for a long-term, committed relationship. Many good friendships have developed this way. If you're not interested in a man, always be upfront about it, but remain kind and sensitive to his feelings. He may really like you and will be hurt. Give yourself enough time to make that determination. Once you realize he's not for you, be honest and move on.

Finally….

Family and relationships are everything and without them, we belong nowhere. Nobody has a perfect relationship all the time. Even the best, most perfectly matched couples have hard times, misunderstandings, and heated arguments.

I hope this guide has not only helped you understand various forms of attachments, but also to appreciate the people in your life and always work towards becoming a better person every single day!

Enjoy!

Thanks for downloading this book. It's my firm belief that it has provided you with all the answers to your questions.

Claim your FREE Audiobook Now

<u>The Confident New You - Develop Your Confidence and Start Living the Life You Deserve</u>

Do you get lost for words around other people, or do you suffer from social anxiety? Are you more concerned about how you look to other people?

If your confidence is always holding you back from achieving what you really want in your life, or if you have always been super shy with no confidence then read on.

You're about to discover how to be confident in any situation. Find out how to make a great first impression and keep the conversation going, without appearing awkward.

Learn to stop thinking negatively about yourself and conquer your fears to gain unstoppable confidence at anything. Even if you don't have low confidence, you can always benefit from improved confidence - there are always greater heights to reach.

THE
CONFIDENT
NEW YOU

DEVELOP YOUR CONFIDENCE
AND START LIVING THE
LIFE YOU DESERVE

DARCY CARTER

www.ingramcontent.com/pod-product-compliance
Lightning Source LLC
Chambersburg PA
CBHW021113080526
44587CB00010B/505